GREAT CHRISTIAN THINKERS

Praise for Other Titles in the Great Christian Thinkers Series

AUGUSTINE Richard Price
'... admirably clear, concise, and though sometimes critical, written with great sympathy and understanding of Augustine's problems, and of the historical context within which he was labouring.' MICHAEL WALSH, *BUTLER'S LIVES OF THE SAINTS* AND *BOOK OF SAINTS*

FRANCIS & BONAVENTURE Paul Rout
'This book meets a real need ... a painless way into Bonaventure's life and thinking, both as a philosopher, a man of prayer and as a great Franciscan.' SISTER FRANCES TERESA, OSC, THE COMMUNITY OF THE POOR CLARES, ARUNDEL

JOHN OF THE CROSS Wilfrid McGreal
'We are greatly indebted to Fr Wilfrid McGreal for bringing alive in such an accessible way the mysticism and mystery of St John of the Cross.' GEORGE CAREY, ARCHBISHOP OF CANTERBURY

THOMAS MORE Anne Murphy
'This superb piece of scholarship sheds new light on the enduring importance of the unity between Thomas More's life and thought. Anne Murphy shows how this large-hearted Christian was a great European and an outstanding example of personal and public integrity.' GERALD O'COLLINS, GREGORIAN UNIVERSITY, ROME

KIERKEGAARD Peter Vardy
'This is a fascinating introduction to Kierkegaard's prophetic insights into the nature of Christian faith, insights which we desperately need to ponder today.' GERALD HUGHES, AUTHOR OF *GOD OF SURPRISES*

SIMONE WEIL Stephen Plant
'Stephen Plant portrays the immense strength and the touching vulnerability of Simone Weil, the complex nature of her convictions, and the startling and continuing relevance of her views today.' DONALD ENGLISH, CHAIRMAN OF THE WORLD METHODIST COUNCIL

AUGUSTINE

Richard Price

SERIES EDITOR: PETER VARDY

270.2
PRIC
c.1

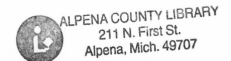

Triumph
Liguori, Missouri

Published by Triumph
An Imprint of Liguori Publications
Liguori, Missouri

Library of Congress Cataloging-in-Publication Data

Price, Richard.
    Augustine / Richard Price. — 1st U.S. ed.
        p.   cm. (Great Christian thinkers)
    Includes bibliographical references and index.
    ISBN 0-7648-0118-X
    1. Augustine, Saint, Bishop of Hippo. I. Title. II. Series.
BR1720.A9P74   1997
270.2'092—dc21
[B]   96-52491

Originally published in English by HarperCollinsPublishers Ltd under the title:
Augustine by Richard Price.

First U.S. Edition 1997
01 00 99 98 97 5 4 3 2 1
Printed in the United States of America

Contents

3-3-98 EP 9.00

Abbreviations

Date Chart

Life of Augustine		General Events	
		258	Death of Cyprian of Carthage
		270	Death of Plotinus
		277	Death of Mani
		312	Start of the Donatist Schism
		312	Conversion of the emperor Constantine
354	Birth at Thagaste in Africa		
		356	Death of Antony of Egypt
373	Read's Cicero's *Hortensius*; becomes a Manichaean 'hearer'		
		374–97	Ambrose Bishop of Milan
384	Goes to Milan		
386	Conversion		
387	Baptized by Ambrose		
387	Death of Monica		
388	Returns to Africa		
391	Ordained priest at Hippo		
395	Consecrated bishop		

Augustine

Introduction

A short book on Augustine is likely to be superficial and will certainly not be comprehensive. The range of his writing covered the whole field of theology, and much philosophy as well. Its sheer bulk is daunting: more of Augustine survives than of any other ancient writer. Nor have his works slept on the shelves through the centuries in dusty repose, for no western theologian has had so strong and wide an influence: he was considered the greatest of the Church Fathers in the Middle Ages and was hugely respected by the Protestant Reformers as well. Attention to his thought has been one of the constant threads in western intellectual history. On a whole range of issues, from the most sublime (the doctrine of the Trinity) to the most earthy (sex and marriage), present-day theologians may disagree with Augustine but cannot ignore him. Disagree they often do. Thomas Allin wrote, back in 1911, 'This great man's influence extended for evil, as his writings show, over practically the whole field of human activity, social and political no less than religious' (*The Augustinian Revolution in Theology*). Such negative judgements, though generally not so sweeping, have recurred throughout this century. At least they serve to keep Augustinian studies alive. Whether or not one likes the ideas of Augustine, everyone with a serious interest in Christian thought has sooner or later to come to grips with them.

Fortunately, Augustine is not only an important writer: he is also a very engaging one, with a style that is both clear and persuasive. No theologian in the history of the Church has been less academic in the bad sense of the word: he was a pastoral bishop who related theological reflections to practical needs, and at the same time a passionate and restless individual, who wrote with a depth and intensity that speak to us directly. A good number of his chief works have been excellently translated into English, and are easier to read than many modern books about him.

Despite the range of his ideas and the breadth of his influence there is a limited repertoire of quotations from Augustine likely at any time to crop up in preaching or popular writing. The two most familiar both come from the *Confessions*, his famous intellectual autobiography; they are worth discussing, since both can be deceptive. Augustine tells us in this work that in his adolescence he used to pray, 'Lord, make me chaste, but not yet' (Co 8.7.17). Very soon he set up house with a mistress with whom he lived for over twelve years. All this can give an impression of an unhealthy personality with an overcharged sex drive, but we need to learn from the historians, who tell us that in Augustine's time living with a mistress was normal and acceptable for a young man on the make, who needed to postpone marriage till he had attained the top of the professional ladder and could marry an heiress (for, as the saying goes, 'don't marry money, but marry where money is'). Less revealing than Augustine's having a mistress is the way he remained faithful to her throughout their relationship. By the standards of the end of the twentieth century the sexual life of the young Augustine was quite unremarkable.

The other all too familiar quotation from the *Confessions* comes on the very first page, where Augustine says to God, 'You have made us for yourself, and our heart is restless until it rests in you.' When a preacher starts off with the words, 'As St Augustine says', in nine cases out of ten this quotation duly follows, as the congregation either purrs or groans. This passage on its own is misleading: it calls up a picture of a sweetly pious Augustine basking in the consolations of religion. But he was at all times an earnest and unquiet spirit; a perpetual seeker, he constantly raised difficult questions and expected no peace till the grave. He also stressed the need to pray at all times and never presume that our salvation is sure.

Those, and they are many, for whom spiritual reflection is primarily an exercise in conjuring up consoling and reassuring fantasies, should be warned off Augustine; but those who appreciate profound and often disturbing reflection on human nature, the workings of God, Christian community, and a host of other vital topics, may be advised to turn to him. I can assure them that they will find much to inspire them and much to infuriate them, and all of it should stimulate them to reflect more deeply on the content of Christian truth and the nature of Christian commitment.

The Path to the Truth

The Conversions of Augustine

Augustine was born in AD 354 in a small town, Thagaste (modern Souk Ahras, in eastern Algeria, forty miles from the sea), in the Roman province of Africa (Tunisia with parts of Algeria and Libya), at a time when the Roman control of the lands round the Mediterranean, and northwards up to Hadrian's Wall and the natural frontiers of the Rhine and the Danube, was still secure. Augustine writes of his parents in terms that reveal a certain coldness towards his father, Patricius, and a close bond with his mother, the pious and possessive Monica. The family was not well off, but the help of a rich neighbour enabled Augustine to proceed, at the age of seventeen, from the usual schooling to the University of Carthage. There he studied the standard subject of Roman higher education, rhetoric – the art of how to speak and write correct and eloquent Latin, on the basis of a careful study of the best literary models. The subject was immensely practical for members of the governing class of the empire and those who hoped to rise into its ranks, since the courtesy and persuasiveness of good Latin prose were essential tools in public life. Augustine did so well at these studies that he went on to teach them himself, holding a series of important chairs of rhetoric at Carthage, Rome, and finally Milan (384–86), which happened at this time to be the seat of the imperial government of Italy and Africa. As the teacher of the sons of the nobility, he could make all the right contacts, and by 386 a provincial governorship and advantageous marriage were pleasantly within reach.

But let us turn from his career to his religious development. His mother was a devout Christian, and enrolled him at his birth as a 'catechumen' in the Church. This meant, strictly, someone enrolled for eventual baptism; but the decision was made to postpone the boy's baptism till he was past the dangerous years of adolescence. Augustine the bishop came to deplore this delay, as implying a lack of faith in the power of the sacrament, but since baptism was understood as not merely a rite of entry into the Church but a solemn undertaking to live a virtuous life, the postponement was certainly prudent. As it was, he grew up connected to the Church by a sort of ethnic loyalty but without committing himself personally.

It was in 373 that he had his first religious crisis, sparked off (oddly perhaps) by one of his set books at university, Cicero's *Hortensius* (written in 45 BC), a call to people to renounce 'the vices and errors of mankind' and devote themselves to the philosopher's quest for truth. The young Augustine did not feel up to self-renunciation – the delights of the flesh and of a growing reputation as a brilliant student were too attractive – but his intellectual interests now took a serious turn. Being a Christian, he first turned to the Bible, which, like many Christians in any age, he had never opened. On finding the contents obscure, contradictory and at times repulsive, he fell easy prey to a semi-Christian sect he happened to meet at just this time, the sect of the Manichees, founded by one Mani in Persia a century before. At no stage of his religious wanderings was Augustine prepared to abandon belief in Christ, but the Manichees professed to be Christians and took a keen interest in the epistles of St Paul (as often, a dangerous sign). Their religion, however, was unlike that of either the Bible or the Church: it taught a radical dualism, or division, between not merely right and wrong, saints and sinners, but between two cosmic principles, of light and of darkness, that eternally confront each other. The teaching of the sect offered an account of the origin, nature and destiny of human beings which expressed rather movingly a sense of alienation in a seemingly oppressive universe. Unfortunately it also suffered from an over-complexity reminiscent of science fiction at its worst.

How could such a system appeal to the young Augustine, and indeed retain his loyalty for a decade? One reason was the sexual renunciation of many members of the sect, which seemed unique to them, since monasticism had not yet reached the province of Africa. Like many young men, he experienced feelings of compulsion and guilt in his own sexual life, and was deeply impressed by chastity. It was a major bonus that, while fully initiated members of the sect had to renounce sex and the world, second-class membership was available to the so-called 'hearers', who admired and assisted the renunciation of the few without having to imitate it; Augustine became one of these, and so was able to continue his career and keep his mistress. Another element in the appeal of Manichaeism was the effectiveness of its attacks on the Church for accepting the whole of the Bible as the Word of God. How could the Old Testament, with its primitive picture of God and shocking stories of debauchery, be part of divine revelation? And the Church defended it not by answering the problems but by claiming a unique authority given by God that excluded rational inquiry. In contrast, the Manichees promised to justify their teachings by reason alone, and their bold and plausible criticisms of the Old Testament seemed a promising start.

As, however, Augustine gradually explored the positive teaching of the sect, doubts set in. When for a time he studied astrology (which, by the way, didn't impress him), he discovered that the astronomical data with which the Manichaean myths were larded were often wildly inaccurate. It was mortifying to discover that Manichaean myths were just as open to criticism as the biblical ones he had rejected in their favour. For a few years (382 to 386) he was in the painful position of having lost faith in Manichaeism without finding faith in any other system.

Fortunately, on arriving in Milan (in 384) he became acquainted with a group of intellectuals who had developed a sophisticated variety of Christianity that combined membership of the Church with a non-literal understanding of the Bible that evaded the criticisms of the literal meaning advanced by the Manichees. This Milanese group interpreted the myths of the Old Testament in the light of Neoplatonism, a development at the hands of Plotinus (third century AD) of the speculations of Plato (fourth century BC) that by Augustine's time had become the dominant form of Greek philosophy. Augustine became a member of this group; for the next few years we may call him a Christian Platonist.

His immediate debt to Platonism was that it cured him of Manichaean dualism. In the Manichaean system good and evil are viewed as two cosmic substances or powers, greater than man, locked in indecisive combat. One effect of this combat is that the 'good soul' within each one of us finds itself imprisoned in a 'Realm of Darkness' that has invaded the 'Realm of Light'. Manichaeism promised that the good soul would eventually be set free and reunited to its heavenly source. The young Augustine, oppressed by a sense of his own wickedness, was pleasantly reassured by a doctrine that attributed moral weakness not to the fault of the individual but to the presence within him of an evil power beyond his control. 'It still seemed to me that it is not we who sin but some other nature sins in us; in my pride it was a great joy to be free of guilt' (Co 5.10.18). But reassurance was bought at a heavy price: if the good is so passive and helpless before the forces of evil, how can one be confident that it will ever be set free?

It was therefore a joy to Augustine to discover the metaphysics of Neoplatonism. This system thought evil not a power or substance on the same level as the good (as in Manichaeism), but something without concrete existence. Whatever is, is good, and 'evil' is simply the absence of good; it can be defined as a deprivation or deficiency, in a being that has become corrupted. Evil is weakness and decay, and we can define it only in terms of the order and harmony from which it is a falling away; it is not some independent power, pitted against goodness in some battle between opposites, as dualism falsely supposes. This notion of deprivation, of evil as loss, appealed strongly to Augustine because it fitted in with his deepest instincts about the nature of moral evil: in choosing the wrong, we are not gaining something positive, that God is rather mean to deny us, but losing sight of real fulfilment, as we become entrapped in compulsive behaviour which cramps and diminishes us as human beings.

In embracing Manichaeism the young Augustine had not thought of himself as giving up Christianity: he had always viewed Manichaeism as a form of Christianity rather than a different religion. And his adoption of Platonism as an answer to Manichaeism does not mean that he now thought Christianity an optional extra: Platonism never claimed to be a self-sufficient system that made religion unnecessary. In the fourth century the choice lay between Christianity and paganism, and paganism had never for a moment attracted him. The decision he made when he finally broke with Manichaeism was to become a member of the Church and embrace the religion of his mother (who had come to Italy to live with him). He made this choice a public commitment by applying for baptism, and receiving the sacrament from Bishop Ambrose of Milan in the following spring (Easter 387).

Baptism meant far more to him than simply joining the Church: he resigned his chair of rhetoric at the same time and gave up his plans to get married. Augustine and the members of his circle felt that the commitment they made to Christ in baptism made it necessary for them to renounce sex and marriage. It is tempting to see this as a lingering inheritance from Manichaeism, but Augustine accepted mainstream Christian teaching on the dignity of marriage. He shared, however, the conviction common to many earnest Christians of the time that baptism means a total commitment to the law of God, a commitment that cannot be fulfilled by those who remain in the midst of the pleasures and distractions of this world. It was this moral earnestness that produced the monastic movement of the fourth century, with its call to give up marriage and property and withdraw from the world; the *Confessions* tell us of the huge impact on Augustine of what he heard at exactly this time of Antony of Egypt and other monastic heroes. In 386 he was converted not to Christianity (he had never ceased to be Christian), and not merely to the faith of the Church, but to a special form of Christian life, based on saying goodbye to marriage and a worldly career.

Set free from worldly responsibilities, he could now devote himself to what he had come to see as his real vocation – the pursuit of Christian philosophy. By this he meant the use of rational argument and concepts drawn from the great philosophers, such as Plato and Cicero, to draw out the Christian sense of human nature as made for union with God. This would be a life's work, and it is to this work that he wished to dedicate himself. There was now no point in remaining in Italy, and by the end of 388 he had returned to Africa. There in his home town, Thagaste, together with friends who had accompanied him to Italy and back, he set up a quasi-monastic community – based on celibacy and a sharing of property, and devoted to prayer, study and discussion. Here, left to himself, he would have spent the rest of his days.

However, with his growing reputation, his literary skills, and his contacts with the imperial court at Milan, he was a prime candidate for a bishopric. People of Augustine's class and background were not supposed to seek office in the Church, but were expected to accept the burden when it was laid upon them. In 391 Augustine visited the port of Hippo (modern Annaba), some forty miles to the north, when looking for a new recruit to his monastery, and was promptly seized and forced to accept ordination – to the priesthood, since the town had a bishop. He put up some resistance, which was expected of someone in this situation. But there is no doubt that he was genuinely overawed at the thought of pastoral office. He was later to speak eloquently of the terrible burden of a pastor, who would have to answer at the Last Judgement not only for his own sins but for those of his flock as well.

The point of making him a priest of the diocese of Hippo was to line him up as the heir apparent of its elderly bishop (one Valerius) before another diocese pinched him. In 395 he was made auxiliary bishop, and on Valerius' death in the following year succeeded to the see. From now until his death in 430 he was tied to pastoral duties in this diocese. We must remember that outside a few great sees bishops were not (as they are today) administrators who delegate the chores of pastoral care to their priests; the priests did not do the bishop's work for him but formed a council to assist him. The bishop remained the father of his flock; he was expected to know them individually, to administer the sacraments (baptism, eucharist, penance), and preach at the Sunday liturgy. He had to attend also to the worldly needs of his flock, representing them in dealings with the state and acting as adjudicator in their civil disputes. One must always remember that Augustine's life was dominated by pastoral duties.

His acute sense of his pastoral responsibilities led him to redirect his intellectual gifts. A few years later (409), and in the not far distant province of Cyrenaica (north-eastern Libya), one Synesius agreed in a similar way to leave the quiet life of a philosopher for the duties of a bishop. He announced in a public letter that he had no intention of abandoning Neoplatonism or of subjecting it to Christian censorship: he would be happy, he said, to preach myths from the pulpit, if he were allowed to pursue truth in his study. Augustine's attitude was quite different. As soon as he became a priest, he abandoned his dreams of a life devoted to philosophy, and immersed himself in the Scriptures. He never shed the basic tenets about God and human nature which he had learnt from philosophy, but from now on he was primarily a biblical theologian, concerned not only to satisfy his own intellect but to serve the Church.

It was this concern for the good of the Church that generated the huge literary production that continued to his dying day: it was to help his flock that he developed his thoughts on Christian teaching, and composed the sermons that form an important part of his literary legacy; it was for the benefit of the faithful, in Africa and beyond, that he produced a huge body of writing to defend the Church against pagans and heretics. We may say that he was primarily a polemical writer responding to the critics of the Church, rather than an academic theologian following his own nose. It is fortunate that he lived in a period when Christian theology was concerned with questions of great practical relevance, and had not degenerated, as it did at times in later centuries, into an academic exercise intended primarily to maintain the status of theologians.

Reason and Authority

It was soon after becoming Bishop of Hippo that Augustine wrote, in the late 390s, the most famous of all his works and the main sources for the earlier part of this chapter – the intellectual autobiography called the *Confessions*. Anyone who has dipped into this work knows that it is much more than an autobiography. Augustine did not write it as a nostalgic exercise in the remembrance of things past, or to satisfy the curiosity of his friends. He saw in his own history a model case of how God humbles and recovers lost sheep; in the course of telling his story he discusses a whole host of theological topics – the powers and defects of the human mind, the need to centre our lives on God, the way to read the Bible, the authority of the Church. Augustine wrote the work as a bishop with a bishop's priorities. The outlook of the book is that of the bishop of Hippo in 397 rather than that of the professor of rhetoric in Carthage and Italy, or of the convert to Christian Platonism of 386.

A case in point is the treatment of Platonism in Book Seven, which treats his intellectual development in the crucial year 386, when Neoplatonism rescued him from the Manichees. Although the creators of Neoplatonism had been pagans, it was quite possible to reconcile it with Christian belief, as many Christian Platonists had already done. As Augustine wrote in the same year:

I am determined never in any way to depart from the authority of Christ, for I have found no stronger one. But as to that which has to be examined by subtle use of the reason – for I long not simply to believe what is true but also to understand it – I feel sure that I shall find it with the Platonists, and that it will not contradict our sacred mysteries. (Ag 3.20.43)

But Book Seven of the *Confessions* is altogether sharper in tone. It uses Neoplatonic ideas to refute Manichaeism, but it pays Neoplatonism no compliments. Instead, it goes on and on about the dangers of intellectual arrogance, by which Augustine means paying more attention to philosophy than the Bible. At the time of his conversion in 386 he viewed Christianity and Platonism, revelation and philosophy, as two parallel sources of wisdom, working together in natural harmony. But by the time he wrote the *Confessions*, eleven years later, he was a Christian bishop who viewed philosophy as useless for the great mass of mankind, who haven't the time or grounding to pursue it, and potentially dangerous for the learned few, who might prefer it to revelation.

Christian heresy too, including the Manichaeism that had entrapped him for so long, was a cautionary tale of what happens when the human intellect neglects the Word of God and sets itself up as an autonomous judge of truth. It was the claim to teach nothing that could not be rationally proved that had first drawn the young Augustine, back in 373, away from the Church to the Manichees:

What drove me to disown the religion which my parents had instilled in me from a child and to be a follower and devoted hearer of those men for almost nine years? It was their claim that we are overawed by

*superstition and told to put faith before reason while they impose faith
on no one without prior discussion to discover what is true.*

This passage is taken from *The Usefulness of Belief* (u 1.2), a defence
of Christian faith that Augustine wrote immediately after his ordination to the priesthood in 391. The book argues that the basis of
knowledge about God is not experience or reasoning but belief
in the teaching authority of the Church. The immediate target
of the book is the criticism of church authority put forward by
the Manichees; but his arguments also apply to claims by philosophers that belief is mere opinion and cannot lead us to real
knowledge. Against this Augustine insists on the necessity of
belief for the attainment of knowledge. In the words of one of his
favourite biblical texts, 'If you do not believe, you will not understand' (ISAIAH 7:9, LATIN VERSION).

How in this work does Augustine defend the claims of authority
and belief, against the rival claim that each individual has the
right, and indeed the duty, to work out his own answers to the
questions of life? He points out that few people have the education
or ability to think philosophically about the existence and nature
of God: are we to deny religion to everyone else? In fact, there is a
whole range of things we all believe without proof. We trust our
friends and colleagues without proof that they are trustworthy.
We honour and obey our parents, yet we know that they *are* our
parents only on the testimony of others. Indeed, we rely on the
authority of others – that is, trustworthy testimony – for our
knowledge about most things.

But why should we trust the Church? Because of 'numbers,
unanimity, antiquity' (14:31). Unlike the various sects, the Church
can claim a consistent teaching tradition going back to the
original apostles of Christ, maintained by an unbroken succes-
sion of bishops throughout the world, and now upheld by
the overwhelming majority of believers. This is not to prefer the
mediocrity of the many to the wisdom of the few, since the Church

can boast generations of holy men and women, virgins, ascetics and martyrs, who prove that the Church is the place where the grace of God is active.

We may allow that this appeal to tradition has a certain force. Augustine was right to feel that in 373 he had been too quick to abandon mainstream Christianity, before he knew much about it, and the same could be said of people nowadays who jettison the faith of their fathers not for solid intellectual reasons but almost casually. Nor can we criticize him for teaching an infantile Christianity, in which the faithful are called to respect the wisdom of their elders and betters for ever and a day, without ever exerting their critical powers: for he held that simple faith is but a first step, and that Christians must aim at developing both their experience and their reasoning powers, in such a way as finally to *know* and *understand* what at first they simply *believe*.

Even so, it is startling to find the size and antiquity of the Church already stressed in the fourth century, at a time when pagans were still as numerous as Christians, and still attacked Christianity as a dangerous novelty. Christian missionaries in the second and third centuries had stressed the rationality of Christianity, against the superstition of paganism, in just the same way that Manichees in the fourth century contrasted their offering of rational proof to the Church's stress on authority. Manichaeism had been fiercely attacked as destructive of tradition by the staunchly pagan emperor Diocletian (284–305), who persecuted Christianity for precisely the same reason. That Christianity cannot defend itself by claiming antiquity was appreciated as late as the 380s by Bishop Ambrose of Milan, who defended Christianity as a new faith that illustrates the law of progress in history.

Augustine's stress on the need to respect authority and recognize the limits of reason was based on more than traditionalism, however: it arose from his faith in Jesus Christ. Now Jesus is a historical figure, who walked the fields of Palestine centuries ago; the life and teaching of the earthly Jesus remain the essential revelation about him even for those who claim spiritual contact with the risen Jesus here and now. We cannot reach Christ through the use of pure reason, since reason cannot uncover the past. Christianity offers not some pure philosophy of timeless truths, but a history of the creation and fall of man, and of the various steps, leading up to the Incarnation, by which God has sought to rescue him. Truths about the past can only be known through authoritative testimony. A Christian has the Bible, but he depends on the teaching of the Church for his knowledge of which writings to regard as inspired Scripture. Of course, such teaching has to be tested on the grounds of its weight and coherence, but in recognizing its authority we are acknowledging the limits of our own experience. The very nature of the Incarnation is a lesson for us: God, in emptying himself to take on human form, above all in undergoing the agony and humiliation of the cross, gives us a powerful lesson in the need for humility.

> *Certain philosophers of this world ... have looked for the Creator in his creation, because he can be found there ... They saw the goal to be reached; but ungrateful to the one who had enabled them to see it, they attributed this vision to their own power. Becoming proud, they failed to attain what they had seen ... They rejected the lowliness of Christ, which would have enabled them, as in a safe vessel, to reach that which they saw from a distance. The cross of Christ appeared sordid to them ... He was crucified for your sake, to teach you humility.* (JG 2.4)

A Manichee, or a pagan philosopher, with his head partly in learned tomes and partly in the clouds, will miss the presence and revelation of God in the dust of Palestine and the empty tomb. We all have a sense of our sinfulness and of our need to be healed if we are to succeed in our quest for God. Philosophers can expand on this with learning and insight, and make us more vividly aware of our spiritual needs. But only the facts of salvation history, accepted on the authority of Scripture and the teaching of the Church, can provide an actual remedy, and point us the way.

> *It is one thing from a wooded peak to catch a glimpse of the homeland of peace and yet not find the way to it and get hopelessly lost, while hosts of deserters from God, under their leader the Lion and the Dragon [the Devil], hem us in and lie in wait for us; and quite another to keep to the path that leads there, under the protection of our heavenly Ruler [Christ].* (Co 7.21.27)

Augustine's intellectual pilgrimage had taught him humility, and this lesson fitted in well with the claims for church authority that came to him naturally once he was a Christian bishop. When as a new convert he had set out to develop a Christian philosophy, he had shown more intellectual openness. His new position as an official apologist for the Church made him more narrowly orthodox, even though his ideas continued to develop. The humility of the convert who accepts authority can begin to look like arrogance and dogmatism, once he comes to serve that authority as its mouthpiece. Augustine the bishop and teacher can easily appear a less attractive figure than the young Augustine seeking the truth. But the energy and urgency of his writing, and its influence on future thought, gained immensely from the fact that he had now to address not the problems he had set himself as an amateur philosopher, but great issues that gripped the Church at large and were to shape the development of Christianity for centuries to come.

(2)

Holy Church and Sinful Members

The creed recited every Sunday in most churches throughout the world affirms belief in 'one holy catholic and apostolic Church'. The choice of adjectives should raise an eyebrow or two. In view of the number of Christian denominations, in what sense is the Church 'one'? Not all churches that reject the authority of the see of Rome are happy to call themselves 'catholic'. 'Apostolic' we can let pass, even though biblical scholars have made it much harder to claim that Christianity as we know it is the same as the religion of the Apostles. But 'holy' is the most problematic adjective of them all: if the Church is a community of saints, what are you and I doing in it? It won't do to say that the Church is holy not in its members but in its doctrines and sacraments, since 'holy Church' means 'the Church of the saints' or 'the holy people'. Christians form a holy people not primarily because of their personal holiness but because they are the people chosen by God, the Holy One; but the phrase is vacuous unless those who make up this people live holy lives.

The Early Church

In fact the early Christians felt no embarrassment in making claims to personal holiness rarely equalled in history. In the words of a text of the early second century,

Christians have the commandments of the Lord Jesus Christ himself engraved upon their hearts, and they observe them ... They do not

commit adultery or fornication; they do not bear false witness or covet the possessions of others; they honour their father and mother, and love their neighbours; they judge justly, and they never do to others what they would not wish others to do to them. (ARISTIDES, APOLOGY 15)

So now you know. If you see a Christian misbehaving, what should you make of it? In the words of Justin Martyr (mid-second century), 'Those who are not found to be living as Christ taught should be regarded as not Christians at all, even if they profess with their lips the precepts of Christ' (FIRST APOLOGY 16). Such passages were propaganda written to impress non-Christians, but they had a theological basis all the same. The Church taught that through baptism and commitment to Christ believers receive into their hearts the Spirit of God, the divine power that makes saints out of sinners. It was hard to see how a Christian who sincerely wanted this grace could fail to receive it. Sanctity, for a Christian, seemed well within reach.

On comparing themselves to their pagan neighbours in the world around them the early Christians enjoyed a very pleasant sense of moral superiority. Although it would be silly to picture the pagan world as a continuous orgy of lust and cruelty, Christians did better than their neighbours in those areas where they developed distinctive standards, notably sex and helping the poor. And they were confident of a huge built-in advantage when it came to religion. Nowadays we tend to think that we have duties towards each other but are free to choose whatever religion we like. In the ancient world, however, everyone – Christians, Jews and pagans alike – believed that justice includes giving God his due, which means worshipping him in the way *he* likes. Christians were sure that only they performed this duty, since the pagans were immersed in polytheism, the worship of false gods, while the Jews, with their curious customs and taboos, were sunk in superstition. Every Christian could say, 'I give alms (sometimes), I make some effort to be chaste, and at least I worship the right God in the right way.' Every Christian could feel that this less than heroic degree of virtue placed him way above his pagan neighbours and earned him the special favour of God.

As a result, early Christians were confident that God listened to their prayers and to theirs alone, and that at the end of time (which they imagined would be soon) Christ would return in glory to reward Christians with the bliss of heaven, and damn everyone else, however virtuous by the world's standards, to the everlasting torments of hell. Some Christians, such as St Paul, were spurred by this thought to feats of missionary heroism, but the great majority found the dreadful fate awaiting their pagan neighbours comforting rather than distressing. The early Christians, perhaps, were not very nice people.

The Church's confidence in the holiness of its members received a rude shock in the middle of the third century, under the pressure of an unprecedented edict issued in 250 by the emperor Decius, which ordered everyone to sacrifice to the pagan gods, and set up bureaucratic machinery to enforce the order. Though many Christians managed to lie low, and a fair number died as martyrs, a very large number conformed to the edict, and later returned to the Church. As a result, the Church's claim to holiness was now somewhat tarnished. The notion of the Church as a community of saints was not abandoned, but the emphasis shifted away from the sanctity of the laity to the need for holiness in the clergy, as the celebrants of the sacraments of baptism and the eucharist. Hitherto the rules for priestly purity in the Old Testament had been taken to express in symbolic form a call to moral perfection addressed to all Christians, the 'priestly' people of God. There were now reinterpreted as referring directly and in their full rigour only to the minister who baptizes, absolves sins, and celebrates the eucharist; it is he who is the 'priest', and the heir of the priests of the Old Covenant.

One of the main participants in the debates of this time of crisis was Bishop Cyprian of Carthage (d. 258), whose writings were regarded in the Africa of Augustine's time as supremely authoritative, second only to the Bible itself. Cyprian held that a bishop or priest who has committed some grave offence can no longer officiate: his sin has deprived him of the Holy Spirit, so how can he give a share in the Spirit to others? The holiness of the laity is necessary for the well-being but not for the existence of the Church; in contrast, the holiness of the minister is essential for the very validity of those sacraments that make the Christian community the Church of Christ.

The Donatist Controversy

More than a century later, Augustine praised Cyprian rather condescendingly as a wise but at times misguided spirit, whose greatest virtue was a readiness to admit he could be wrong (which one wouldn't guess from his writings). His teaching had come to the fore again as a result of a disastrous schism that occurred in the African Church early in the fourth century.

In 312 one Caecilian, who had made enemies by trying to undermine the reverence paid to martyrs, got himself hastily consecrated bishop of Carthage (and therefore the chief bishop of Roman Africa) before his opponents had time to assemble. They responded by contesting his election on the grounds that one of the bishops who had taken part was a *tradidor* ('hander over'), that is, had compromised himself in time of persecution by handing over copies of the Scriptures to the pagan authorities – an offence that counted as apostasy (betraying the faith). They therefore set up as rival bishop the deacon Majorinus, who on his death soon afterwards was succeeded by Donatus. Soon all Africa was divided into supporters of Caecilian and supporters of Donatus.

Caecilian had been consecrated first, and the argument against the validity of his consecration was doubtful both on point of fact and on point of law; as a result he gained the recognition of all the churches outside Africa. This enabled him to claim the title of

'Catholic' bishop, while his opponents were merely 'Donatists'. (Note, by the way, that when I use the word 'Catholic' in this book it will normally follow this ancient usage, where 'Catholic' does not mean 'Roman Catholic', as opposed to 'Orthodox' or 'Reformed', but refers to the universal Church of the early centuries, from which all modern Christian denominations derive, and excludes only such small schismatic groups as the Donatists.)

The Donatists retaliated by condemning the churches that accepted Caecilian: by this act they had condoned the sin of *traditio* ('handing over') and therefore shared in its guilt; this excluded them from the true Church of Christ, which was now reduced to the Donatists themselves. Like the fond parents watching a military parade who exclaimed, 'Only our Johnny is marching in step', the Donatists refused to be browbeaten by a mere number count, and indeed within Africa itself they remained strong, perhaps even outnumbering their opponents; by the time of Augustine every town in the province had rival Catholic and Donatist bishops. Clumsy and sporadic attempts to suppress Donatism on the part of the state authorities served only to reinforce Donatist self-identity as the church of martyrs, opposed to the church of *traditores*, dependent on the powers of this world. The first three centuries, when Christians were a despised and persecuted minority, had left their mark: even Augustine in the early fifth century instinctively viewed the Church as a holy remnant that would always be liable to harassment.

But Augustine's own allegiance to the Catholic Church was never in doubt: after his years in Italy Donatism appeared insufferably provincial, and its claim to be the one true Church of Christ merely silly. Already as a priest in Hippo (where Donatists at first outnumbered Catholics) and then as the chief propagandist for all Catholic Africa, he produced over a period of thirty years a whole √ series of works reiterating patiently, if monotonously, the great lines of the anti-Donatist cause. Like so many who take part in public controversy, he had limited freedom to choose his ground:

the debate had been defined, the battle lines drawn up, decades back. After years as a professor of rhetoric he was well able to argue the case, indeed almost any case, with confidence.

Since the writings of the Donatists themselves are lost, it is all too easy to accept his arguments uncritically. If the Donatists had survived down to the modern age (in fact they disappear from history with the Muslim conquest of Africa at the end of the seventh century), ecumenical courtesy would make us try to grasp their point of view. As it is, the great majority of modern commentators take it for granted they they had not a leg to stand on. This makes it seem that Augustine was labouring the obvious. It is worth making the effort to understand his opponents in order to make the debate interesting again. I should warn my reader at this point that the dispute was highly involved and the arguments often devious; if you have no taste for the niceties of theological debate, I would advise you to skip on ahead to the next section, 'Mixture in the Church'.

One of the points in the debate was the problem of rebaptism. What is the status of schismatic baptism, that is, baptism performed by groups like the Donatists who have separated themselves from the main body of believers and are therefore guilty of the sin of 'schism' (splitting the Church)? Are their baptisms valid, or should schismatics received into the Church be baptized again? By Augustine's time all western Catholics accepted the validity of schismatic baptism, including the baptisms performed by the Donatists; but the Donatists themselves imposed rebaptism on those Catholics (schismatics in their eyes) who came over to them. Augustine tells us that this Donatist practice, while criticized by many as fanatical, caused agonies to the scrupulous, and tempted some Catholics to receive Donatist baptism, since everyone recognized it, and then return to the Catholic fold. This gave pastoral urgency to his arguments on behalf of schismatic baptism. (Note the irony of the situation: Augustine defended schismatic baptism not out of a wish to be nice to schismatics but in order to defend Catholic baptism against schismatic attack.)

The rite of baptism is regarded by most Christians today as a ceremony of thanksgiving to God and of admission into the Church. But the early Christians had a much more dramatic view of baptism: they saw it as a radical transformation, by which the candidate is freed from the Devil, receives the Holy Spirit into his soul, is united to Christ as a member of his 'body', and adopted as a child of the Father. The Church is the community of those who are sanctified by the Spirit and made members of the holy people of God. This raises the question: is it possible to receive the grace of baptism outside the one true Church? Is schismatic baptism valid? The debate first flared up in the middle of the third century when, in the wake of persecution, a significant number of Christians were baptized in schism and then sought readmission into the Church. Were they, or were they not, to be baptized again? Cyprian was certain that they were, and argued the case cogently. The whole teaching of the New Testament presumes that the Church is a united, harmonious community. As the 'body of Christ' – the community sanctified and inspired by the risen Christ – it cannot lose the unity it possesses in him. Schism cannot split the Church: it merely separates schismatics from the Church. Since the fruit of the Spirit is love and peace, those who have rejected their fellow Christians by going into schism have rejected the Spirit; as a result they can neither bestow nor receive the Spirit.

Pope Stephen of Rome (d. 257), however, rejected Cyprian's arguments. Treating the two parts of the rite of baptism (the pouring of water and the anointing with oil) as two separate sacraments, he argued that the anointing confers the Holy Spirit, while the washing of baptism is merely for the forgiveness of sins: unlike the anointing it does not confer the Spirit and therefore it can be validly performed outside the Church. The argument was hopelessly askew, since the notion of a valid forgiveness of sins without the gift of the Holy Spirit is theological nonsense: St Paul clearly links forgiveness of sins to union with Christ, and union with Christ to receiving the Spirit. It is ironic that the whole

21

subsequent practice of western Christendom, where each denomination recognizes the baptism of the others, derives from this unsatisfactory ruling of Stephen's.

By the time of Augustine the Catholics in Africa had adopted the Roman position, while the Donatists remained faithful to that of Cyprian. Augustine, fortunately, did not repeat the arguments of Stephen. Instead, he introduced a rather contrived distinction between validity and effectiveness: baptism can be validly performed outside the Church, but it only begins to take effect and to benefit the recipient when he returns to the Catholic fold. Baptism outside the Church does not produce a single one of its fruits; nevertheless, it is valid and unrepeatable.

But what of the argument that baptism outside the Church cannot be valid since the Holy Spirit cannot be bestowed by one who, as a schismatic, has cut himself off from the Spirit? This brings us to the central issue in the Donatist controversy: can the sacraments of baptism and the eucharist be validly performed by a minister in a state of 'mortal' sin – that is, by a priest who has sinned so gravely as to expel the Spirit he received in baptism and cause the 'death' of his own soul? The whole basis of the Donatist schism was that the Catholic bishops throughout the world, having once condoned *traditio*, had been deprived of the Spirit, and therefore had nothing to bestow on either their flock or their successors in the episcopal office. The notion of guilt by association has never, perhaps, been exploited so absurdly. The Catholics in response not only defended the worthiness of their own bishops but also attacked the theological tenet fundamental to their opponents' case – the invalidity of sacraments performed by unworthy ministers. Against this they made a claim that must have made Cyprian turn in his grave: the state of grace of the minister is entirely irrelevant for both the validity and the effectiveness of the sacrament. This was the position that Augustine set out to defend in the most important of his anti-Donatist treatises – *Baptism: Against the Donatists*, written in 400–1.

Augustine makes great play of the presence within the Church of people who are Christians 'in words rather than actions', and no more in a state of grace than the schismatics; yet no one doubts their ability to give, as to receive, baptism. If the validity of a sacrament were made to depend on the spiritual state of the celebrant, we could never be certain that we had been validly baptized or validly absolved from our sins; the sacramental system set up by Christ must have a surer foundation. But does Augustine's conclusion follow? Consider, for example, the case of a celebrant who makes a serious mistake in reading out the set prayers. The standard principle is that the sacrament is nevertheless valid, since 'the Lord supplies'. But this doesn't mean that the validity of the sacrament has nothing to do with using the right words. Similarly, why not say that the normal working of a sacrament requires a worthy minister, but that the Lord supplies when the minister is unworthy? This would surely be better than to say with Augustine that the worthiness of the minister is wholly irrelevant, and that the Holy Spirit works not through the heart and mind of the celebrant but merely through his outward words and gestures.

In the mainstream churches today it is generally held that all that is necessary for the validity of a sacrament, apart from the correct ritual, is a right intention on the part of the minister – that is, he must intend to perform the sacrament. But Augustine is reluctant to admit even this: after all, in the case of an unworthy minister who has no part in the Holy Spirit, it is difficult to be confident of the rightness of his intentions. This drives Augustine to the extreme position that the correct words and gestures may possibly be adequate even when there is no intention to perform the sacrament at all. He raises as a genuine problem the validity or otherwise of a baptism performed 'in jest, as in a comedy', when neither baptizer nor baptized has serious intentions or even the faith (BAPTISM 7.53.101). Despairing of finding a theological answer, he comes up with the astonishing proposal that the only

23

way to solve this baffling puzzle, as he sees it, is to pray for a special revelation from heaven. A theology of the sacraments that produces a 'problem' such as this stands self-condemned. How could validity depend on correct ritual alone and not at all on the intentions of those taking part? This would reduce the whole sacramental system to a form of magic.

Mixture in the Church

If there was no more to Augustine's contribution to the Donatist controversy than this, it would not deserve a chapter, but fortunately he developed a further argument that is far stronger and of much greater interest.

As we have seen, the Church of the first three centuries saw itself as a community of saints. Historians used to think that all this, and much else besides, went out of the window at the conversion to Christianity of the emperor Constantine in 312, as a result of which floods of dubious converts poured into the Church and corrupted it. But this picture is rejected by scholars today. In fact the conversion of the Roman world was a gradual process, and the Church was careful not to lower its standards; the penances imposed, for example, on grave sinners remained long and severe.

Donatism has often been described as a puritanical movement that wanted to exclude sinners from the Church. This reflects Augustine's own rhetoric rather than the facts of the case. Donatists had the same attitude as Catholics to the failings of the laity; they did not imitate the rigorist Novatianist sect which, in the time of Cyprian, had declared that those who committed grave sins after baptism had to be excluded from holy communion for life. Instead, as we have seen, the Donatists, as the heirs of Cyprian, concentrated on the need for holiness in the ministry. In practice this was not specially demanding, since it consisted of little more than the furious condemnation of a sin of *traditio* committed in unrepeatable circumstances decades before. But at least the Donatists preserved the self-identity of earlier Christians, with their stress on the purity of the Church, as an 'enclosed garden' set apart from the corruption of the world.

It was this traditional stereotype, preserved so rigidly by the Donatists, that Augustine set out to destroy. He quoted with relish the numerous passages in the writings of Cyprian on the deplorable state of the Church at the time of Decius' persecution (250), and used them as evidence that the Church is not a community of saints. Cyprian himself would not have liked his rhetoric being taken so literally; but complaints of the lukewarmness of Christians, and their failure to live up to their baptismal promises, were just as common in the early centuries as in later ones – a fact ignored by those church historians, both ancient and modern, who romanticize the primitive Church. Augustine built on this fact to make the strong claim that the Church is and always has been full of the spiritually dead, who have no share in the Holy Spirit; indeed, these, according to Augustine, are 'the many', while the righteous are 'the few'.

Again we meet the notion of the holy remnant, but he does not identify it with the Church, nor with a particular section of the Church: we shall not know till the Day of Judgement who for certain are the righteous and who the unrighteous, who (to use the biblical imagery) are the wheat and who the chaff. All we know is that both are to be found within the Church. This state of affairs is actually, Augustine argues, part of God's plan for the good of the Church, since it enables the righteous to develop the virtues of humility and tolerance. What is strikingly absent in this and similar passages is any anxiety about contamination, any fear that the presence of so many sinners might deprive the Church of its very identity; and yet this fear had been strong in the primitive Church, with its concern to maintain a clear boundary between holy Church and wicked world.

Equally notable is the stress Augustine places on an intermediate class of believers – those who are still in their sins but with God's grace are gradually advancing towards holiness. It is not even necessary for them to reach this state in the present life: on condition that they are moving in the right direction, they will be saved. For many individuals, as for the Church as a whole, the path through this world is a pilgrim state of slow, often imperceptible, progress in which backsliding and renewed repentance are a constant fact of life.

What, then, do we mean when we call the Church 'holy'? Augustine's favourite answer is to distinguish between the church community as a social entity on earth and the holy Church of those destined by God to join the communion of saints in heaven: it is possible to say that sinners only *appear* to be members of the holy Church. Does this mean that there are really two Churches – the visible Church with its hierarchy and sacraments and an invisible Church of saints? This was how many of the sixteenth-century Reformers understood Augustine; but it is not what he meant. In his view the public sacraments of the Church, performed by the clergy, do not indeed convey salvation to everyone who receives them, but there is no salvation without them: we cannot turn our backs on the visible Church and claim to belong to an invisible one. Cyprian had written, 'You cannot have God for your Father if you do not have the Church for your mother' (THE UNITY OF THE CATHOLIC CHURCH 6). For Cyprian as for Augustine the Church is the visible Church, despite the presence within it of unworthy members who will not accompany the saints into heaven.

But Augustine came to yet a deeper understanding of the presence of sinners in the Church – the 'mixture' of saints and sinners, as he liked to call it. He came to see that this mixture is not just an unfortunate accident, due to human failings, but belongs to the very essence of the Church, as the community of men and women who have been called to holiness but are still sinners. Those in the Church who are destined for salvation are indeed God's 'elect' (chosen ones), but none of them is free from sin in this age. A common need to recognize their sins unites all members of the Church, sinners and 'saints' alike.

The whole Church says, 'Forgive us our trespasses.' This means it has stains and wrinkles. By confession the wrinkle is smoothed out, by confession the stain is washed away. The Church stands in prayer in order to be cleansed by confession; and as long as it lives in this world it stands like that. And whenever somebody departs from the body, all his sins are forgiven, at least those capable of being forgiven, through the daily prayer of the Church. And then he departs cleansed, and the Church is stored up in the Lord's treasury as pure gold. This is how the Church enters the Lord's treasury without stain or wrinkle. (S 181.5.7)

So it is all the members of the visible Church, including the elect, who need day by day to pray for forgiveness. And when God forgives the sins of his elect, it is in response to the prayers not just of the elect themselves but of the whole Church. Furthermore, just as the elect depend on the prayers of all, so they depend on the sacraments and the preaching performed by all the ministers of the Church, worthy and unworthy alike. The Church remains holy in that it is the ark of salvation, whose prayers and sacraments are the channels of divine grace; but the holiness is not the scrupulous purity of fastidious souls who shun the company of sinners.

Even Christ, the only sinless man (in Augustine's view) who has walked this earth, took on himself the burden of the sins of the world; in the startling words of Scripture, he 'was made sin for our sake' (2 CORINTHIANS 5:21). Christ's cry of despair from the cross, 'My God, my God, why have you abandoned me?' (MARK 15:34), is interpreted by Augustine as the anguish of a sinful world, that Christ takes upon himself. There is, then, a deep solidarity that binds Christ to sinners in this age; in Christ's own words, he came to call 'not the righteous but sinners' (MATTHEW 9:13). We may even say that a 'perfect' Church would not be the Church that Christ died to found.

The Church has strong members, and it also has weak ones. It can't do without its strong members, and it can't do without its weak ones ... because without both of them there is no Church. (S 76.3.4)

In all, Augustine was calling on the Church to develop a new identity: the Church's traditional view of itself as the holy remnant in the midst of a sinful world had to be abandoned. In issuing this call, he was pressing for a change that was in fact achieved through a gradual evolution – the slow process by which, over many centuries, the Christian community ceased to be the small, self-righteous sect it had been in the age of the Apostles, and grew into the Church of the Middle Ages and of modern Europe, keen to embrace all men and women who at least recognize Christian values, and realistic in the demands it makes upon them.

In calling for this change, Augustine was not merely saying that Christians ought to stop giving themselves airs; nor did he point out, as a modern historian would, that in the conditions of a Christian empire the character of Christianity was bound to change. The heart of his picture of the Church lies instead in profound theological reflection on the incarnation of Christ. In 'emptying' himself to become a human being in this fallen world, and in 'humbling' himself to accept death, even death on a cross (PHILIPPIANS 2:6–8), Christ gave an example of solidarity with sinners that must be imitated even in the holy Church of God: if Christ bore the sins of the world, we too must 'bear' (tolerate) sinners. If the Church were to seek to exclude them, it would not secure but lose its holiness, because it would have ceased to follow its divine Lord. As in Augustine's arguments against pagans and Manichees, so at the heart of his case against the Donatists lies the paradox of the humility and humiliation of the incarnate and crucified God.

3

Church and World

If the Church itself is a mixed body, this is bound to affect its attitude to the society around it. In political terms this is the problem of the relationship between Church and state. This is another area where Augustine's influence down the centuries has been enormous. His thoughts on the matter were developed in response to some of the most dramatic events in the whole of European history. In his youth the Roman empire, stretching from Britain to the Sahara, from the Atlantic to Mesopotamia, seemed as secure as ever. The emperors were Christians, and by the end of the fourth century had prohibited pagan worship. It was natural for Christians to suppose that under the protection of the one true God the empire would now go from strength to strength. But Augustine lived to see Britain, Gaul and Spain overrun by barbarian invaders, and as he lay dying in 430 his own city of Hippo was under siege by the Vandals.

Augustine and the Sack of Rome

The most traumatic moment in this sudden collapse of Roman power in western Europe was the sack of Rome by the Goths in 410. This was not in itself the fall of the empire: the Goths soon left Italy for Gaul; and Rome, though still officially the capital of the empire, had long ceased to be the centre of government. But the sack came as a terrible shock to all who still looked at the city as the symbol of Roman power and Roman civilization. Refugees, fleeing before the Goths, circulated their tales of woe round the whole empire. The reactions of many were eloquently expressed by Jerome, the great translator and commentator of the Bible: 'Oh horror! The world is collapsing in ruins. The renowned city, the capital of the Roman empire, is destroyed in one tremendous fire, and there is no part of the earth where there are not Roman exiles' (LETTER 128:4). 'If Rome can perish, what can be safe?' (123.17).

But a Christian's feelings towards the city of Rome were likely to be very mixed. On the one hand, it was the capital of an empire that no one wished to see collapse in chaos. But on the other hand its great days of glory had been as pagan Rome, the persecutor of the Church, glutted with the blood of the martyrs. The conversion of the empire (or at least the emperors) to Christianity had put an end to persecution, but injustice and corruption were just as prevalent as before.

The traditional attitude of Christians to the Roman state had been critical but nuanced. The books of the New Testament vary enormously in the attitude they express towards Roman power. At one end of the spectrum we have St Paul insisting that the state authorities are established by God and are his 'agents working for your good' (ROMANS 13:4); at the other, we have the Revelation of John, with its tirades against Rome the New Babylon, the whore drunk with the blood of the saints. The same range of attitudes continued in Christian writing till the time of Constantine (d. 337), the first Christian emperor: on the one hand, the empire was welcomed as a gift from God that secured peace round the Mediterranean and so helped the spread of the gospel; on the other hand, in pursuing its own godless aims and demanding the obedience of its subjects, it looked like a satanic parody of the true empire, the kingdom of Christ. Although in any one Christian writer of this early period one of these views is likely to be dominant, it is misleading to treat them as mutually exclusive. In fact, they were really two sides of the same coin. Yes, God had given world power to the Romans, for the benefit of the Church. But at the same time the Romans worshipped the pagan gods – in the Christian view, real but demonic spirits who set the state against the Church. The reaction of Christians was to maintain an attitude of cautious reserve. The state had its uses, and was better than anarchy. But its value was only provisional: the eyes of faith were set on the return of Christ in glory, when the true kingdom would come and Roman power, indeed all worldly authority, vanish away, like dew at the rising of the sun.

At the end of the second century the African writer Tertullian wrote, 'The emperors too would have become Christians, if either the world had not needed emperors, or Christians could have become emperors' (*APOLOGETICUM* 21.24). But in the fourth century the incredible happened: the emperors became Christian, from Constantine onwards. This did not immediately make Christianity the 'state religion', but it transformed its prospects. Most of the emperors keenly promoted the power and status of the Church, while imposing increasing restrictions on pagan worship. By the time of Augustine's death the Greek-speaking half of the empire (Greece and the Near East) had developed a new nationalism, based on belief that the true God and the Christian empire were the closest of allies: if the empire maintained the true faith against the enemies of God, pagans and heretics, God in his turn would give the empire victory over its enemies.

The attitude of Christians in the western, Latin-speaking half of the empire was more reserved. The Church was very conscious of the benefits it now received from the state, and its members had no desire to be swamped by barbarian hordes. But older attitudes of disapproval and distrust died hard. There were a number of reasons for this. Paganism remained stronger than in the east, and prevented a sense of identification between the Christian community and society at large. Moreover, patriotism was generally weaker in the west than in the east: no one welcomed the barbarian invasions, but no one was ready, either, to pay for an army adequate to drive them back. There was no patriotic wave of opinion to swing the Church away from its traditional attitude of cautious reserve towards the state. As a result this attitude was modified but not abandoned.

We have seen how Jerome was deeply shocked by the sack of Rome by the Goths in 410. Augustine's reaction was more nuanced. He had none of the sentimental attachment to the 'eternal city' of those who venerated its past, but on the other hand he felt pity for the victims of the sack and was sensitive to the distress the news caused his flock in Africa. As the leading apologist for the Christian cause, he had to refute the arguments of the pagans: it seemed to them, and to weak Christians too, that the cause of the disaster was the prohibition of pagan cult; the pagan gods had protected Rome in the past and were now punishing it for its apostasy. There was also puzzlement among pious Christians at the occurrence of such a disaster in 'these Christian times': why was God not looking after the empire, now that it was no longer the enemy but the friend of the Church?

Of course there had been similar disasters in the past, and similar debates. In the middle of the third century the empire had been devastated by a combination of plague, bad harvests and barbarian invasions. Pagans accused Christians of causing these disasters by their refusal to worship the gods. Cyprian of Carthage (d. 258) reacted with a defence little calculated to appease the opposition:

> No one should suppose that the Christians are not proved right by the events taking place because they suffer from them just as much as everyone else. World catastrophes feel like a punishment to people who find happiness and glory only in the world ... But the disasters of the present time do not upset those whose hope lies rather in the good things to come. Misfortunes do not overwhelm us or break us or distress us, nor do we moan over any turn of events or state of bodies. Living by the spirit rather than by the flesh, we overcome weakness of body by firmness of soul. We are utterly confident that the very things that torment and try us prove and strengthen us. (TO DEMETRIANUS 4)

Augustine now put forward similar arguments. Surely, he urged, it is short-sighted and unspiritual to whine about earthly misfortunes. Loss of property, even of life itself, should not distress immortal souls: the only secure and lasting goods are moral integrity and the reward that awaits it in heaven. All misfortunes pale before eternal damnation, the fate in store for the enemies of God.

In this reaction traditional Christian narrow-mindedness was reinforced by philosophical clap-trap about the indifference of the wise man to the misfortunes of the body. We can scarcely blame Augustine, with his late Roman and early Christian background, for falling back on these inadequate platitudes: we all grasp at straws when disaster strikes. But he was a man of broader sympathies than Cyprian, and in the predominantly Christian society of late-Roman Africa it was not possible for Christians to pretend that they were a sect set apart, for whom national disasters were of no concern. Augustine realized that the crisis of the empire had opened up the whole question of the attitude of Christians towards state and society, towards the pagan heritage of Rome, towards the distinctive interpretation of history inherited from the Bible. To cope with all these questions, he embarked in 413 on what, by the time he completed it in 426, had become the longest and richest of all his works (more than 1,000 pages in a modern edition) – the *City of God*.

The Two Cities

The work could have been called (to anticipate Charles Dickens) *A Tale of Two Cities*. It contrasts at length the history and destiny of the 'city of God' and the 'earthly city'. The use of the word 'city' derives from scriptural texts such as Hebrews 13:14, 'Here we have no lasting city, but we seek the city which is to come.' The city of God, or 'heavenly city', is made up not only of the saints in heaven but also of all those human beings on earth who are true members of the people of God. The basic distinction between the two cities lies in the difference in the objects of their love.

The two cities were created by two kinds of love: the earthly city was created by self-love leading to contempt for God, the heavenly city by the love of God leading to contempt of self. In fact, the former glories in itself, the latter glories in the Lord. The former seeks glory from men, the latter finds its highest glory in God, the witness of a pure conscience. In the former the lust for power dominates over both its rulers and the nations it subjugates; in the latter both serve one another in love, the rulers by their guidance, the subjects by obedience. The former loves its own strength shown in its powerful men; the latter says to its God, 'I will love you, Lord, my strength.' (C 14.28)

In other words, the citizens of the heavenly city live as exiles and pilgrims upon earth with their sights set on the world to come. In contrast, the earthly city is built up by ambitious men whose aim is to dominate their fellows. Its citizens make self-gratification their goal in life, the more gifted pursuing power and fame, the majority pleasure and wealth.

Careful scholars have pointed out that the distinction between the city of God and the earthly city is not the same as that between 'Church' and 'state'. The distinction between the two cities is a distinction not between two organizations but between two states of mind. Augustine traces the distinction to before the Church appeared on the scene, indeed all the way back to Cain and Abel (the sons of Adam and Eve in biblical mythology): the murderer Cain was the founder of the earthly city, while righteous Abel was the first citizen of the heavenly one. Moreover, the concept of the 'state' familiar to us is a development of the later Middle Ages, centuries after Augustine. When we think of the 'state', we think of an autonomous secular sphere with its own place in the natural, God-given scheme of things; it is necessarily distinct from the Church, since it is not run by church officials and has different goals. But Augustine is not thinking of administrative structure, and he does not acknowledge the existence of a secular sphere that has a right to develop secular values distinct from the law of God. The earthly city is, simply, mankind in rebellion against God.

Once we are clear that Augustine is not discussing the relation between Church and state as understood in later political theory, it is safe to admit that the two pairs of terms, though distinct in meaning, tend in practice to coincide. In the final section of the preceding chapter we saw how Augustine had no wish to draw a sharp distinction between the institutional Church and a spiritual Church of the saints. It is true that within the Church a distinction exists between its true members and false brethren, but the two cannot be told apart in this life, and are intimately linked together by the bonds of Christian fellowship. The fact that the Church on earth is a mixed society of saints and sinners does not prevent it from 'being even now the kingdom of Christ and the kingdom of heaven' (C 20.9). Similarly, when Augustine writes of the earthly city, he is usually thinking of the Roman empire, except when he is discussing the pre-Roman past. In all, in Augustine's own world the distinction between the city of God and the earthly city effectively coincided with that between the Church and the Roman state.

The *City of God* offers an interpretation of Roman history indebted to the pagan historians (notably Sallust, first century BC) who had been critical of Roman imperialism, but gives it a new theological slant. Augustine's account runs as follows. Back in the early days of the Roman Republic, God decided to give world power to the Romans, that is 'to those men who sought honour, praise and glory in serving their country, did not hesitate to put their country's safety above their own, and who suppressed greed for money and many other vices in favour of that one vice of theirs, the love of praise' (C 5.13). Thirst for glory gave birth to 'lust for power' (a phrase Augustine took from Sallust), and the Roman empire expanded steadily, until at the time of Christ's birth it included the whole Mediterranean world. By that time the lack of a serious external threat had long sapped the sinews of the Roman spirit, and moral corruption had infected the whole of society. The ruling class wallowed in luxurious living and political infighting; the mass of the population was kept quiet by the amusements of the theatre and amphitheatre, whose sex and sadism pandered to its lowest instincts. Having rejected God's law, the Romans had no defence against the demons, who are the true objects of pagan worship and relish human wickedness. Polytheism and moral corruption marked the earthly city as clearly as worship of the one true God and obedience to his law marked, and mark, the heavenly one.

The fourth century had seen the arrival on the scene of Christian emperors and the destruction of the power of paganism. Did this mean the situation had radically changed? Was there reason to hope that in a Christian empire the state would cease to embody the earthly city and become instead the political organ of the city of God? Augustine was wisely sceptical. For one thing, it was too early in the early fifth century to be confident that the triumph of the Church would be permanent; persecution might return. But there was a more fundamental objection: the triumph of the Church did not mean the sanctification of the human race. Life was still to be lived in a fallen world among fallen human beings.

Augustine did not expect this to change. This was because, following biblical teaching and early Christian tradition, he accepted that the righteous will always be a small remnant in the world. The Fall has corrupted human nature, and divine grace rescues only a few. The righteous are a minority even in the Church, though thanks to them the Church continues to promote Christian values; but in the world at large they will never be able to dominate society. Human society as a whole, and the political states that administer it, will continue to form part of the earthly city, dominated by love of self and contempt for God.

Christians in the World

If, then, the state is irredeemable, what attitude should Christians have towards it? Should they detach themselves and avoid direct involvement? In the Church before Augustine's time Christians had been strongly discouraged from volunteering for public service, whether in government or the army. What place can gospel values have there? It might appear that in the world of public action Christians will always be out of place, like fish out of water.

But in Augustine's world Christians did not form a separate group. They had to take part in the life of the broader society. How could the Church, itself a mixed body of saints and sinners, look with contempt on the earthly city? In so far as the earthly city is the Roman commonwealth, all the members of Augustine's flock belonged to it; in its stricter definition as the world in rebellion against God, the unrighteous in the Church are its secret members. Mixture within the Church itself contributes to the subtle bond between the two cities. 'In fact', as Augustine wrote, 'these two cities are mixed up and entangled with each other in this age, and will only be separated at the Last Judgement' (C 1.35).

What makes up civil society? As Augustine points out, Cicero in his political treatise *The Republic* (written in the 50s BC) had defined it as 'the association of a multitude of rational beings united by a common agreement on the objects of their love'. Do members of the city of God on earth have any aims in common with members of the earthly city? Augustine replies that they do: we all equally want 'peace', that is, friendly and mutually helpful relations with our fellow men and women. This common interest enables practical co-operation, although, of course, differences remain.

The household of human beings who do not live by faith aims at an earthly peace based on the good things of this temporal life; but the household of human beings who live by faith does not let itself be

*distracted by these things from its journey towards God, but treats
them as supports with which to endure and keep within check the burdens of 'the corruptible body which weighs down the soul [WISDOM
9:15]. In this way both kinds of human beings and both households
share the use of the things we need in this mortal life, but each has its
own very different end in using them. So too the earthly city aims at
an earthly peace, and establishes an agreement between its citizens as
regards authority and obedience, in order to achieve a certain harmony of human wills as regards the things of this mortal life. But the
heavenly city, or rather that part of it which is on pilgrimage in this
perishable world, is also obliged to make use of this peace, until the
passing away of the perishable world for which this kind of peace is
essential. And therefore it does not hesitate to obey the laws of the
earthly city which regulate those things which help to sustain mortal
life.* (C 19.17 ABRIDGED)

Augustine's argument that Christians should collaborate with the
broader society is hard to fault; less welcome is his teaching that
they should conform to the laws and customs of that society. He
had no sense that Christians should have their own distinctive set
of political and social values. He was saddened by the harsher
aspects of life in the Roman empire – external and civil wars, the
regular use of torture in criminal trials, the institution of slavery.
He looked forward to their disappearance in the world to come,
but he could not imagine life in this world without them. In a
fallen world full of vicious human beings he saw no alternative to
a hierarchical society that uses violence both to repel its enemies
and to impose obedience on its members.

How could this be squared with Christ's Sermon on the Mount,
with its rejection of the use of force even in self-defence? 'I order
you not to resist the wicked; but if anyone strikes you on the right
cheek, turn to him the other also' (MATTHEW 5:39). Augustine
argued that this text is concerned not with acts but attitudes:
human beings often have to discipline the weak and foolish,

punish the wicked and repel their enemies, but this they must do in a spirit not of brutality or revenge but of concern for the common good. It is not even necessary for the servant of the state to convince himself that each recourse to force is necessary: since the maintenance of state authority is necessary for the general good, he is right to obey orders as they stand, and leave it to his superiors to answer for them before God. He has a duty to disobey only those orders that are directly contrary to religion.

It would be unfair to say that Augustine was complacent about the harshness and cruelty of the late Roman state: he placed it high among the trials and tribulations that make us despair of happiness in this life and yearn for the life to come. But he did not think that this created any real problem of conscience for the earnest Christian engaged in government service.

The Christians of the first three centuries had tended to steer clear of involvement in public life. This was mainly due to the difficulties in serving a pagan state, but also to the Christian ideal of detachment from the sordid affairs of this passing world, as we saw illustrated in Cyprian. This misplaced otherworldliness survived the coming of Christian emperors: the popes of Augustine's time included state service as among the dangerous professions forbidden to those who were doing penance for their sins or who had already done penance. This negative attitude to state service, surprising in a now Christian empire, received a fresh impetus from the monastic movement of the fourth century: many able men who would previously have gone into public life left society for the desert, or at least the service of the Church; Augustine himself was of their number. This makes his encouragement of Christian lay people to serve society and promote peace in the world much more than the platitude it may sound to us today; here again, as in his teaching on the Church as a mixed society, he was moving it away from its sectarian origins and towards a proper understanding of its role in society. This is the positive side of his social and political teaching. The negative side, as we have seen, is an excessive political conformism. But this is a fault that can be charged against the overwhelming majority of Christians throughout history. In pressing the charge we must be careful not to blame Augustine for conforming to the ideas of his own day while we are equally uncritical of the ideas of our own.

Coercion of Heretics

As we have seen, Augustine did not suppose that the arrival of Christian emperors meant the advent of the kingdom of God. But he did recognize that it helped the Church. Not only were the centuries of persecution at an end (at least temporarily), but state law was now available for the promotion of true religion. By the end of the fourth century the emperors had destroyed the power of pagans to molest the Church. Why not complete the good work by crushing enemies who were still more dangerous – schismatics and heretics, who used the name of Christ to draw Christians away from the true fold? This leads us on to a notorious topic where Augustine was criticized in his own day and has been widely condemned since – his defence of state coercion of heretics.

Here again he was responding to events and did not choose his ground. In a series of edicts, dating principally to 405 and 412, the Roman state, at the request of the African bishops, tried to force the Donatists to give up their schism and submit to the established Church: their churches were confiscated, their services were banned, their clergy were threatened with exile, and their laity with heavy financial penalties, if they did not return to the Catholic fold.

When coercive measures were first proposed, Augustine had opposed their introduction: he did not think that error had any rights, but he was afraid that the Church would be unable to absorb a flood of reluctant converts. But he now changed his tune, partly because as an official apologist for the Church he had no option, and partly because the converts turned out better than he had expected.

My original opinion was that no one should be forced into the unity of Christ: there should be attack in word, battle in argument and victory through reason, lest those we had known as open heretics should be landed on us as insincere Catholics. But this opinion of mine was overcome, not by the arguments of opponents but by factual proofs. What proved me wrong above all was the example of my own city, which, though formerly entirely in the Donatist party, was converted through fear of the imperial laws to Catholic unity ... People were so helped by the terror of these laws that some now say, 'We already knew this to be the truth, but we were held back by some habit or other; thanks be to God, who has broken our chains and transferred us to the bond of peace.' Others say, 'We did not know this to be the truth and were not ready to learn it, but we have become keen to learn it out of the fear of losing temporal goods without gaining eternal ones; thanks be to God, who used terror to dispel our negligence and to make us seek out anxiously what in time of security we never wanted to know.' Others say, 'We were deterred from entering by reports whose falsity we only learnt on entering, and we needed coercion to make us enter; thanks be to God who used this whip to teach us how false and empty were the lies people told about his Church.' Others say, 'We thought it did not matter where we practised Christianity; but thanks be to God who rescued us from schism and showed us that the one God is to be worshipped in unity.' (L 93.4.17–18)

Augustine found support for the use of coercion in Scripture itself. God had constantly driven the Israelites to repentance by punishing them. The conversion of St Paul, overwhelmed by a heavenly vision on the road to Damascus, was a still better example of how God acts: he does not wait humbly on the sidelines and *ask* human beings whether they want to be converted. So in the case of heretics it is quite inadequate to say that people must be left to find their own way to the truth: they may in their present situation lack both the opportunity to encounter the truth and the ability to recognize it when they do. Of course it would be better for them to discover the truth on their own initiative, but often this is not possible. Their freedom is adequately respected if, after being forced to assent to the truth, they come to believe in it genuinely; their belated consent makes up for the initial use of coercion.

In the parable of the Great Banquet (LUKE 14:16–24) God is compared to a host who sends out his servant to the highways and hedges to *compel* people to come in. As Augustine commented,

> *They stick in the hedges, they don't want to be compelled. 'Let us enter,' they say, 'of our own will.' This was not what the Lord ordered: 'Compel them', he said, 'to come in.' Let necessity be experienced from without, and consent is born within.* (S 112.7.8)

These passages represent Augustine at his best and at his worst. His defence of a policy of state oppression which drove many Donatists to suicide borders on the obscene. Moreover, his argument has thoroughly unpleasant implications: once you start persecuting erroneous views, where do you draw the line? In the later Middle Ages and the time of the Reformation his arguments were eagerly exploited by pious fanatics who wished to impose their own version of Christianity by means of state law. At the same time, however, his defence of the coercion of heretics shows real psychological insight: in our permissive society we are all too well aware that untrammelled 'freedom of choice' can enslave people to social or psychological pressures where no choice worthy of the name is actually exercised.

It is painful to read that his arguments were later used to defend such horrors as the Inquisition. But this should not blind us to the sheer logicality of a policy of coercion, once it is assumed, as most Christians did assume as late as the eighteenth century, that everyone who dies in heresy or schism goes straight to hell. We do not respect freedom of choice when it leads to drug-taking or drunken driving, yet schism in Christian eyes is far more destructive than either. If salvation is through faith in Christ and if Christ founded the one true Church as the ark of salvation, what ground do Christians have for tolerating other religions or for allowing a plurality of denominations? The arguments for religious coercion can appear perfectly, indeed horribly, logical.

It was not till the Second Vatican Council (1962–65) that the Roman Catholic Church attempted the difficult task of reconciling modern ideas of religious freedom with its traditional claim to be the one true Church. The *Declaration on Religious Liberty*, one of the most impressive of the council documents, argues that the service of God is only possible where there is freedom from coercion, since 'the practice of religion of its very nature consists primarily of those voluntary and free acts by which a human being directs himself to God' (1.3). Augustine would have said that this teaching is far too abstract and ignores the concrete situation – the lack of human freedom as a result of original sin and social pressures. It is to his teaching on original sin, and on the work of divine grace to restore freedom of the will, that I shall now turn.

4

Freedom and Grace

Pelagius

I would imagine that for at least a century every student of theology, at some stage in his or her course, has written an essay on why Pelagius was a heretic. And yet almost none of these students actually read Pelagius: after all, his surviving writings have only recently been translated. Nevertheless, they were expected to condemn him without a hearing; not even the Inquisition was so unjust. In a broader context Pelagius often used to be mentioned as the typical Briton – a staunch active Christian, indifferent to such theological subtleties as the notion of divine grace, little given to the passive religiosity of depending on God, but confident in the strength nature has given him, and keen to realize the pious maxim, 'God helps those who help themselves'.

But first some facts of biography. Pelagius was born in Britain at around the time of Augustine's birth (354); Jerome could later describe him as having 'wits addled with Scotch porridge'. He settled in Rome in the early 380s. There he became a leader of the new ascetic, or monastic, movement. This movement primarily attracted noble ladies, widows and virgins. Though some of them gave their wealth to the poor (to the protests of their relatives), most held on to it and used it for good works, such as building up around them communities dedicated to prayer and Scripture study. In contrast to the ostentatious consumption and mild debauchery of many Roman aristocrats (so brilliantly satirized by

Jerome), they formed a very self-conscious élite. Pelagius became the spiritual director of many of these ladies, and wrote in beautiful Latin how right they were and how wicked was the life they had renounced. Just before the sack of Rome by the Goths in 410 he and several of his followers fled to Africa. Within a year he had moved on to Palestine, but his disciple Caelestius sparked a rumpus in Carthage when he tried to spread the views of his master.

Following Pelagius, Caelestius denied that the Fall of Adam had radically altered the human condition. In effect he denied what came to be called 'original sin', a doctrine particularly loved by the African church. According to this doctrine, mankind as a whole has inherited from Adam the terrible consequences of his sin – the inability to do right, and mortality experienced as not a mere fact of nature but a punishment. Since baptism, in the view of the African church, is the remedy for original sin, this teaching seemed to deny the need for baptism; in this case, the whole debate with the Donatists over when and where baptism is valid and effective had been a total waste of time. Such subversive teaching could not of course be tolerated: the African church duly condemned Caelestius as a heretic.

The matter was taken up in Palestine, where Pelagius was now staying, and there in 415 a council at Diospolis, without looking deeply into the matter, gave him the benefit of the doubt and declared him free of heresy. The African church renewed its anathemas, and Pope Zosimus (417–18) was obliged to adjudicate; sadly he disgraced the Roman see first by acquitting Pelagius and Caelestius, and then by reversing this verdict under political pressure, when the African bishops successfully lobbied the imperial court. Pelagius himself now disappears from history, but the debate rumbled on, right up to Augustine's death (430) and beyond.

The term 'Pelagian' means someone who thinks that human beings can obey God's law without the help of his grace. Was Pelagius a Pelagian? He was certainly no theologian, merely a fine preacher and an effective spiritual director; his mauling by Augustine is like a butterfly being broken on a wheel. But his views represent an interesting stage in the developing idealism of the ascetic movement of the fourth century. The core of his message is that Christians are called to perfection and are capable of attaining it. It is unfair to say that he thought unaided human nature sufficient. He acknowledged the truth of a theme found also in Augustine: bad teaching and worse example over countless generations have corrupted human society, creating a habit of sin that has become second nature. We need the law of God and the example of Christ to teach us the way; we need the free forgiveness of past sins bestowed in baptism to fire us with confidence and gratitude.

But Pelagius firmly rejected the view that the Fall of Man has left us with a weakened and corrupt nature that no effort of the human will can restore, even guided by the law of God. He saw no merit in the notion that freedom from sin requires an additional, inner grace, a change of heart and will that only God can bring about. Such views seemed to him to subvert moral effort; salvation consists not in piously twiddling one's thumbs waiting for an extraordinary gift of grace, but in an active and generous response to the call of the gospel.

In many respects the teaching of Pelagius was a genuine continuation of early Christian teaching, with its stress on the free commitment to a pure and holy life that a Christian takes on at baptism. But his insistence that perfection is possible and therefore obligatory goes well beyond the less exacting standards of the Church of the first three centuries, which was satisfied if converts avoided the grossest sins such as idolatry and adultery. His demand that we obey the whole law of God reflects the moral earnestness of the ascetic movement of the fourth century. In his own conversion back in 386, Augustine had embraced the same ideals; but after years of fighting the Donatists he had come to accept a mixture of saints and sinners in the Church and had no time for spiritual élitism.

Augustine on Grace

The Donatist controversy had established Augustine as the principal propagandist of the African church, and as early as 412 he was called upon to attack the new enemy. Pelagius' final defeat in 418 did not close the debate, which continued right down to Augustine's death in 430. It was increasingly fed by Augustine himself, as he drew out more and more the logic of his anti-Pelagian position and developed an extreme stance that shocked many of his former allies.

We saw how in the Donatist debate Augustine inherited the main lines of controversy and had limited freedom of manoeuvre. In contrast, the challenge of Pelagius was one he would have been happy to dream up: the field was new, and the topic one that had been of deep concern to him long before he had even heard of Pelagius. It had been at the centre of his thought since 396, when at one of the turning points of his intellectual development he finally saw the full force of St Paul's Letter to the Romans: 'Wretched man that I am, who will set me free from the body of this death? The grace of God through Jesus Christ our Lord' (ROMANS 7:24–25, LATIN VERSION).

The *Confessions* (written in the late 390s) have plenty to say about the limitations of human freedom and the need for divine grace; 'Give what you command, and command what you will', is a leading theme of Book Ten, and implies already that the law itself, which Pelagius thought the main instrument of grace, is inadequate to change hearts. In contrast to Pelagius' insistence on the power of the human will, Augustine's account of his conversion brings out the impotence of the will, which only attains freedom when liberated by divine grace:

You, Lord, are good and merciful. You turned your gaze on me, sunk in death, and with your right hand drew out the pit of corruption at the bottom of my heart. As a result I ceased to want what I had wanted

before and came to want only what you wanted. Where had my free
will been for so many years? Out of what deep hiding-place was it
suddenly called forth? (Co 9.1.1.)

Pelagius thought this rhetorical and perverse. There seemed
nothing in Augustine's conversion that his own theology could
not explain. Corrupt culture and sensual indulgence create a
habit of sin that is hard to break; but this habit can be broken by a
free and spontaneous decision of the will when the soul is fired by
the word of God – in Augustine's case the reading of the Letters of
St Paul in the months immediately preceding his conversion. But
Augustine saw in his long enslavement to sex and ambition not
mere habit but the power of original sin – that radical corruption
of human nature which we all experience and can trace back to
our common ancestors, the first human pair, Adam and Eve.

The story of the sin of Adam and Eve that led to their expulsion
from Paradise (the 'Fall of Man', as it came to be called) is a multi-
layered myth that has a variety of meanings even in the original
text of Genesis, to say nothing of the wealth of interpretation it
received in the early Church. Augustine's interpretation of the
story has dominated western reading of it ever since, to the extent
that it needs a careful study of the text to realize how many other
interpretations are equally possible.

According to Augustine, Adam and Eve before the Fall enjoyed
privileges scarcely believable in human beings. They were free of
complexes and irrational drives; they possessed a deep knowledge,
and exercised a control, of the natural world; they enjoyed a
relationship with God as close as that of the angels. They were far
more exalted beings than the virtuous cavemen in whom conser-
vative Christians of our own day believe, in a rather comical
attempt to reconcile Genesis with modern views of the prehistory
of the human race. But all these wonderful privileges were for-
feited as a result of the Fall, when man lost not only the delights of
Paradise but also the original harmony of his being. Fallen man

has a natural love of self, not of God; and he is full of irrational drives, specially of sex and aggression, that prevent him from pursuing the good. He still possesses freedom of the will, in that he makes conscious choices; but in practice he is only able to choose evil. Augustine refused to be impressed by the moral heroes of pagan antiquity: their apparent virtues were merely 'magnificent vices', for they were not motivated by a love of God.

In view of the total depravity of fallen man, the remedies of divine grace, as described by Pelagius, seemed woefully inadequate. The Law of God and the example of Christ may possibly fire us with a desire to do good, but in fallen men this desire need not lead to action at all, still less to a consistent life of virtue. As Augustine had learnt from earlier experience, you can long to change your life without having the strength to do so. Divine grace in the Augustinian scheme, like a doctor using every drug in his bag, has to make simultaneous use of a variety of remedies. With those who are particularly resistant, there is no alternative to the major surgery of a divine miracle that shifts and redirects the deepest drives of the will – as in the case of the conversion of St Paul on the road to Damascus, who set out as a rabid persecutor of Christians and was then literally stunned by an act of God. Once there is some spark in us able to respond to God, grace has to fan that spark into life by bringing the right external influences to bear and enabling us to respond to them.

> *'The free choice of the will is very powerful', you say, but what power does it have in the case of those sold under sin? ... We are ordered to believe, so that by receiving the gift of the Holy Spirit we can do right actions out of love. But who can believe unless he is moved by some call, that is, by some kind of evidence? Who has it in his power to ensure that his mind attains just the right perception to move his will to faith? Who can respond enthusiastically to something that does not delight him? Who has it in his power to ensure either that he will meet what can delight him or that it will delight him when he meets it?* (Si 1.2.21)

Even when the will is strongly drawn to right action, it meets the resistance of contrary drives and habits. God has to complete his 'operation' that inspires the will by his 'co-operation' that gives the will the power to progress from desire to effective action.

He who wishes to keep God's commandments but is unable to do so already possesses a good will, but as yet a small and weak one ... And who was it who gave Peter the first small portion of the gift of love but he who both prepares the human will and perfects by his co-operation what he initiates by his operation? He begins by operating in us to give us the will, and completes it by co-operating with us when we have the will. (G 17.33)

God is not merely a skilful physician of souls: he is a master of his own creation, and nothing can frustrate his will. His will to save includes the 'gift of perseverance', that is, a special grace to ensure that those chosen by God do not fall away from him. No one can achieve this of his own will: it comes from God as pure gift. Augustine's final position, as set out in *The Gift of Perseverance* (written in 429), is that our contribution to our own salvation consists of praying for this gift, and of nothing more: everything else is the work of God. As Augustine insisted again and again, human beings are totally dependent on God and stand before him as the humble recipients of his grace, not as the moral heroes who have achieved their own salvation and can look God firmly in the eye.

Augustine's critics accused him of treating human beings as passive pawns and denying the freedom of the will. But the whole point he was trying to make is that freedom of the will is itself the gift of God, who restores to human beings both the ability to choose the good and the power to achieve it. The texts I have quoted illustrate Augustine's acute perception of how the human will actually operates. God's grace does not compel the will to obey him automatically, like a cog in a machine; instead, it elicits a spontaneous response by means of an inspiration given to man as a conscious and rational being.

Predestination

Against the Manichees, Augustine had insisted that human beings are not the helpless playthings of embattled cosmic powers: evil has no real existence, and man possesses free will. The Pelagians claimed that in his attacks on them he had gone back on this. Certainly he stressed different aspects of the truth in different contexts, but he had a coherent position none the less.

It can be summed up as follows. Man in his fallen state is only capable of evil, but God is able to rescue him, not by overriding his free will but precisely by empowering it. Evil is not something concrete and positive, but a mere deficiency, an absence of the good. Every created being in virtue of his mere existence has some share of the good; every conscious and rational being has some potential to respond to the grace of God. In fallen man this potential is so weakened as to be wholly dormant. But divine grace is able to bring this potential to realization, to reawaken and re-animate the natural powers within the soul of every human being; this it does by acting through both external stimuli and inner assistance within the will itself. As beings endowed with free will, we could choose to resist the healing action of God; but God can so work on us that we have not the faintest inclination to exercise this freedom. The salvation of the whole human race is something easily within the capacity of the divine will. Grace (if it choose) is irresistible.

Does this mean that every single human being will be saved? Such 'universalism', as it is called, seems to have been held by Origen of Alexandria (d. 254), the greatest Christian thinker before Augustine, and appeals, of course, to many Christians today. It could surely draw powerful reinforcement from Augustine's doctrine of the irresistibility of grace. But in fact Augustine is the very last theologian universalists think of appealing to, and for a very good reason. Augustine thought universalism quite impossible, whatever one's theology of grace. For him it was ruled out by one simple fact – what happens at baptism. The early Church proclaimed, following the gospel (JOHN 3:5), that only the baptized could be saved. It is a simple fact that not all are baptized. It followed necessarily that not all are saved; hell and damnation are the destiny of a large part, indeed the greater part, of the human race.

This conclusion is so unattractive to us today that it needs to be explained in greater detail. The stress on the absolute necessity of baptism, while very understandable in the wake of the Donatist dispute, would generally be rejected today, and was questioned by some of Augustine's contemporaries. They tried to exploit the traditional idea of 'baptism of desire', that is, a love of God equivalent to the commitment entered into at baptism: those who have this desire and yet (through no fault of their own) fail to be baptized will still be saved. Augustine resisted this line of escape; he came to recognize only baptism by blood, that is, a martyr's death, as an adequate substitute for baptism in water.

This was arguably too restrictive, but there is good biblical support for insisting not perhaps on baptism but at least on the gift of God associated with baptism – the gift of faith. The New Testament insists again and again that faith in Christ is essential for salvation; it does not hold out salvation for those (the majority of the human race) who do not commit themselves to Christ. Admittedly, this stress on the need for a conscious commitment to Christ goes against Augustine's own stress on the unconscious springs of the will, which are deeper than our choices; and Augustine was well aware that a 'conscious commitment' does not necessarily indicate a real consent of the heart. But he was sufficiently loyal to church tradition to steer clear of any suggestion that there might be a Christianity of the heart without conscious Christian belief.

A further problem for universalism lies in the biblical theme of the holy remnant, chosen by grace (e.g. ROMANS 11:5). A constant theme of the Bible is that most of mankind, even of God's own people, wander off after false gods, leaving behind only a tiny body of faithful. Those invited to the wedding feast scorn the invitation, for many are called but few are chosen (MATTHEW 22:2-14). The notion of 'grace' in early Christian thought was linked to notions of 'favour' and 'privilege'; it was contrasted to the concept of the 'natural' good that all human beings possess in virtue of their creation.

In Augustine's own day universalism was not an issue at all. All Christians agreed that only members of the one true Church could be saved, and that not even all of them would be saved: God 'elects' (chooses) the recipients of his mercy and makes them members of the Church, where they mix with fellow Christians who are called into the Church but not chosen for salvation. The only question was the relationship between human choice and divine election. Does God choose his 'elect' in virtue of their merits, already existent or foreseen? Or is election a wholly unmerited gift? Is the saving grace of God irresistible and only bestowed on a few, or is it offered to all and rejected by most?

Augustine's opponents liked citing the saying of St Paul, 'God our Saviour wants everyone to be saved and come to know the truth' (1 TIMOTHY 2:4). They rejected Augustine's argument that, if salvation was offered to all, God's mercy would be displayed but not his justice. For God's justice has been fully satisfied by the death of Christ: in the words of St Paul, 'one has died for all and therefore all have died' (2 CORINTHIANS 5:14). In other words, Christ took on himself the penalty for our sins, and we no longer have to pay it ourselves. Instead, all human beings are offered sufficient grace for salvation. The gospel is offered to all; its truth is clear from the wisdom of its teaching, its spread throughout the world, and the miracles and personal holiness that have attended it. All have the opportunity to respond to the gospel; if nevertheless they fail to attain salvation, this is not God's will but their own choice.

Augustine attacked this position as contrary to his deepest convictions about both God and human beings. Many who reject the gospel, or who fail to live up to it, never possessed the perception and the self-control necessary to make it a real option for them. To say that God wants to save everyone but can't achieve it is to deny his power and resourcefulness: how could any creature resist a creator determined to use every means to ensure his salvation? The fact that human beings have free will means that divine grace has to operate in a particular way; it does not make that grace ineffective. The verse from the First Letter to Timothy is certainly awkward, but it simply cannot mean what is seems to mean. Any fool can quote a verse of Scripture; only a wise man can interpret it. The fact that Christ paid the penalty for sin enables God to be merciful to those he chooses, but does not oblige him to show mercy to all.

A special problem arose from the fate of infants who died before baptism: it seemed unjust to send them to hell when they hadn't had the chance to be baptized. A popular solution was to suppose that God foresaw that if they had been baptized they would have failed to live up to the grace of baptism, and therefore killed them off before they disgraced both themselves and the sacrament; but their foreseen misdeeds remained adequate to justify their damnation. This argument received from Augustine the scorn it deserved. It is an affront to justice, he argued, to suggest that unbaptized infants are condemned for sins they never had the chance to commit. Their damnation can only be explained as the penalty for the sin they were born with – the guilt that each one of us inherits from Adam: he left us not only a corrupt and tainted nature but also a heavy burden of guilt, which we call 'original sin'.

Augustine claimed that all human beings in some sense 'sinned in Adam' and share in his guilt; they therefore deserve damnation even if, like unbaptized infants, they have committed no sins of their own. This argument builds on the notion of a natural solidarity between descendants and ancestors, or more generally between human beings linked by history. None of us exists apart, limited to the little world of our own personal choices; apart from the life of individuals, there is the sharing of individuals in a common life, where we must accept responsibility for the sins of the society of which we are members. As a rebuttal of the extreme claims of modern individualism this belief of Augustine's in human solidarity has much to be said for it. But whether this solidarity is sufficient to justify eternal damnation for those who die without committing sins of their own is, of course, another question. It is one where Augustine's position is particularly hard to defend.

It was not only the problem of unbaptized infants, however, that made Augustine stress original sin. Since he was sure that God is able to save whomever he pleases, and yet believed that not all are saved, he concluded that God does not wish to save everyone. How is this compatible with the Christian conviction that God is love? Augustine argued that because of the guilt of original sin every-one deserves eternal damnation. The amazing thing is not that many are damned but that any at all are saved. While damnation of the many is required by the justice of God, the salvation of the few is proof of the depths of his mercy. God does not choose to damn anyone: in the case of the majority he simply allows the effect of sin to take its natural course. Meanwhile, he shows his love by rescuing the few; he uses all the resources of his grace to ensure their salvation, despite the effects of original sin.

God's decisions are never reactive but creative. He chose his elect before they were born, indeed before the world was made, and it is this original choice that we call 'predestination'. The long course of human history is the working out of that original design; in the words of St Paul 'those whom he predestined he also called, and those whom he called he also justified, and those whom he justified he also glorified' (ROMANS 8:30).

What guides God in his selection of the predestined? Does he choose those who, he foresees, will prove themselves worthy? This answer was, of course, quite impossible for Augustine; for all are equally unworthy, and the virtues we see in some of our Christian brothers and sisters are not the *cause* of God's choice but its *fruit*. We seem reduced to saying that God's choice is simply arbitrary. In fact Augustine draws back from this unattractive conclusion. He plays with the unhappy idea that divine justice may be different from, and superior to, human ideas of justice. He insists that God must have good reasons for making the selection he does, even if these reasons are for us an inscrutable mystery, hidden in the secret abyss of divine wisdom. All this is theological gobbledy-gook for 'I haven't a clue'. Augustine's inability to answer this crucial question is yet another weakness in his theory. The doctrine of predestination, after all his efforts, turns out to be incoherent as well as repulsive.

A Dubious Legacy

Augustine's doctrine of original sin built on the work of certain of his predecessors, notably Tertullian of Carthage (*c*.AD 200), who had introduced the idea that the sinfulness of Adam is passed on to his descendants not merely by bad upbringing and social influences but by the very act of procreation. It is this view of original sin that demands the historicity of Adam as the common ancestor of the whole human race; in contrast, most early Christian interpretation of the Adam story treated him as primarily a symbol of the human race as a whole. Augustine not only adopted Tertullian's picture but developed its blackest traits: the notion of inherited guilt sufficient to justify eternal damnation was the happy invention of Augustine himself. The very term 'original sin' was probably coined by him, and it was through his influence that a strong doctrine of original sin became part of the common inheritance of western Christendom.

The idea of strict predestination was also an innovation of Augustine's. It upset many of his contemporaries and has remained highly contentious ever since; no part of his legacy has been more fiercely attacked. The claim that God wills the salvation of only a few of the members of the Church threatens his own doctrine of the solidarity between saints and sinners (see chapter 2 above), even though he tried to evade this by stressing our ignorance of who is, and who is not, among the elect. The notion of predestination, in a loose sense, as an expression of our confidence in God's power to save, was traditional and uncontroversial, but as developed by Augustine in the context of a strong doctrine of original sin and our dependence on grace it became virtually a new doctrine. In the later Catholic tradition Augustine was honoured as the 'theologian of grace' but his teaching on predestination was watered down or simply ignored. It was the reformer Calvin in the sixteenth century, and then the Catholic Jansen in the seventeenth, who revived the full Augustinian doctrine and brought it back to the centre of theological debate. The Roman Church condemned Jansen, and tried hard to pretend that this left Augustine himself unscathed.

The philosophers of the eighteenth-century Enlightenment could be more frank. Voltaire, in the article 'Original Sin' in the 1767 edition of his *Philosophical Dictionary*, described the doctrine as 'the wild and fantastic invention of an African both debauched and repentant, Manichee and Christian, tolerant and a persecutor, who spent his life contradicting himself'. Voltaire reacted strongly against the Augustinian inheritance; he rejected the whole set of notions that Augustine had spent his best years defending. Original sin, predestination, eternal damnation – all these went out of the window. For Voltaire, human beings are born with a pure and untainted nature:

> *Gather together all the children in the world, and you will find nothing in them but innocence, sweetness and modesty. If they were born wicked, criminal, and cruel, they would show some sign of it, just as baby serpents try to bite and baby tigers to tear. But nature, having created man, like pigeons and rabbits, without weapons of attack, has not implanted in him any destructive instincts.* (PHILOSOPHICAL DICTIONARY, 'WICKEDNESS')

It is only bad education and corrupt social influences that produce vice and crime. And just as human beings are naturally loving and lovable, so God himself is pure benevolence, and loves all mankind equally. There is no distinction between the order of grace and the order of nature: God bestows his love on all his creatures, not on some special class of the elect. Baptism does not bestow special privileges on the baptized but celebrates the universal gift of birth.

It is because the 'heresy' of Voltaire has become the orthodoxy of liberal Christianity, or virtually so, that strong doctrines of original sin and predestination appear so monstrous to modern believers. Most theologians would like to jettison the more negative aspects of Augustine's position while preserving many of his insights on the human will and the workings of grace. A tart judgement would be that in his writings on grace he is good on how the will operates but poor on the purposes of God – in other words, that he was a better psychologist than he was a theologian. His doctrine of original sin is repulsive to those who assert the goodness of human nature as created and sustained by God; but after all the murders and assaults we read of every day in our newspapers, let alone the death camps of Hitler and Stalin and the other horrors of twentieth-century history, we must surely concede that Augustine was more realistic than Voltaire about human nature.

To return to Augustine's own context, let us note how his reaction to Pelagianism was in many ways an extension of his battle against Donatism. Both Pelagians and Donatists proclaimed a Church 'without spot or wrinkle', a holy remnant uncontaminated by the world. Augustine did not abandon the notion of a holy remnant, but he reduced its impact by stressing the weakness of all human beings, even the elect, and their dependence on divine grace at every stage of their existence. The gift of perseverance gives no ground for feelings of superiority, since no one can tell till he dies whether or not he has received it.

The Christian apologists of the first three centuries had stressed our freedom to embrace the gospel and commit ourselves to Christ with confidence: once baptism has freed us from the sin and blindness of our former life, we possess the power to remain true to that commitment. Augustine too was a firm believer in the power of baptism, but not because it conquers sin in one fell swoop: rather, it starts us on a long and painful pilgrimage, and gives us the grace we shall need every step of the way. The Church is less the haven of the reborn, radiant with spiritual health, than a hospital where the best we can do is submit to treatment.

There are people, ungrateful towards grace, who attribute much to our poor and wounded nature. It is true that man when he was created was given great strength of will, but by sinning he lost it. He fell into death. The robbers left him on the road half-dead. A passing Samaritan lifted him onto his beast of burden. He is still undergoing treatment. 'But sufficient for me,' someone says, 'is what I received in baptism – forgiveness of all sins.' But surely the destruction of wickedness does not mean the end of weakness? ... You will remember, beloved, the man half-dead who was wounded by robbers on the road, how he is consoled, receiving oil and wine for his wounds [the Parable of the Good Samaritan, LUKE 10:30-37]. His sins, it is true, were already forgiven; and yet his sickness is cured in the inn. The inn, if you can recognize it, is the Church. While in the inn let us submit to treatment; let us not boast of health while we are still weak ... Say to your soul, say this: you are still in this life, the flesh is still weak; even after complete forgiveness you were prescribed prayer as a remedy; you still have to say, until your sickness is cured, 'Forgive us our trespasses'. (S 131.6.6)

5

Sex and Marriage

Augustine's teaching on original sin, discussed in the last chapter, had a particular influence on his view of sex and marriage. This subject relates as well to another key theme of this book – the holiness of the people of God. Obviously a concern with holiness makes people morally scrupulous. But there was more to it than that: the ideas connected to holiness in the early Church produced a particular form of sexual morality, new in the ancient world.

Early Christians and Sex

The early Christians prided themselves on being the holy people of God; they claimed a unique relationship with God in heaven as members of his holy Church. This gave them an inner sense of unique status in the unseen world. Inevitably this contrasted strongly with the visible reality of everyday life, where Christians had many of the same concerns as their pagan neighbours and didn't seem so very unusual, apart from their strange religion. The problem became: how were Christians to embody their inner holiness in their outward lives? How best could they express their sense of a special identity? The Church very soon came to concentrate on one area of conduct which seemed to give special scope – sexual behaviour. In the words of the brilliant contemporary historian Peter Brown,

On the surface the Christians practised an austere sexual moral-
ity, easily recognizable and acclaimed by outsiders: total sexual

renunciation by the few; marital concord between spouses ... strong disapproval of remarriage. This surface was presented openly to outsiders. Lacking the clear ritual boundaries provided in Judaism by circumcision and dietary laws, Christians tended to make their exceptional sexual discipline bear the full burden of expressing the difference between themselves and the pagan world. (A HISTORY OF PRIVATE LIFE, P. ARIÈS AND G. DUBY, EDS, 1.263)

To modern Christians this stress on sexual purity seems unbalanced, even unhealthy, and they will wish that the first Christians had made a different choice. But their choice is easy to understand if we look at their social setting and ideology. For one thing it gave equal scope to all: not everyone has the means to give alms, not everyone has a job where he can prove his honesty and public spirit, but everyone has to cope with his or her sexuality.

But there were solid theological reasons as well. On the level of ideology, there was the language in the Bible about spiritual rebirth. 'In baptism you have been raised with Christ through faith in the working of God who raised him from the dead' (COLOSSIANS 2:12). This spiritual entry into heaven, this gift of new life, is bestowed not through physical procreation but through the new birth of baptism. Even in this age Christians share in the gifts of the age to come: what could be more appropriate than to anticipate that age by renouncing marriage, or at least remarriage, here and now? In the words of the gospel, 'The sons of this age marry and are given in marriage, but those deemed worthy to attain that life and the resurrection from the dead neither marry nor are given in marriage' (LUKE 20:34-35).

On a deeper level than that of ideology, the attitude of Christians towards the body was strongly influenced by their feelings about the Church. Social anthropologists have taught us how closely attitudes to the physical body reflect attitudes towards society, the social 'body'. The early Christians wanted to maintain a clear boundary between themselves and the pagan world around them;

they were concerned to preserve the purity of the Church as the 'body of Christ'. It was natural that this concern should spill over into an anxiety about the purity of their own bodies. Early Christians felt a need to express and preserve the purity of the Church through the bodily purity of its members. To maintain itself as a heavenly society in exile upon earth, the Church needed members whose own bodies stood apart from the blurring and contamination brought about by easy sexual relations. This did not necessarily mean rejecting marriage: it did mean a new stress on sexual morality, and a stiffening of the rules.

These various motives in favour of a strict sexual morality cut little ice with Augustine: as we saw in the *City of God*, he was realistic about our need to accept the conditions of life on earth and the intimate links between Church and world. But there was a third motive that appealed to him powerfully – the ideal of single-mindedness. Many of Jesus' parables, such as the parables of the people who sell all they have in order to buy the pearl of great value or the field with treasure in it (MATTHEW 13:44-46), have as their message the ideal of single-mindedness or purity of heart. St Paul used this ideal to encourage celibacy: 'The unmarried man cares about the affairs of the Lord, how to please the Lord; but the married man cares about the affairs of the world, how to please his wife, and he is split in two' (1 CORINTHIANS 7:32-34).

In early Christianity (as in the Platonism which influenced Augustine so strongly in his youth) moral evil was seen as loss of unity, through the loss of rational control over man's instinctive drives, particularly those of sex and aggression. Self-control could be compared, as in Plato's *Republic*, to the political control exercised by the state: the edicts of rulers receive the rational obedience of their subjects. But in man the irrational drives (or 'passions') are, by definition, incapable of rational obedience. Some early Christian moralists, such as Clement of Alexandria, urged Christians to stamp out the passions altogether. Others recommend what we today would call sublimation – preserving the energy of sexual desire but channelling it into love for God. But the standard teaching of the Church was more realistic: the sexual drives are to be contained within marriage.

What is the essential purpose of marriage? Jewish and Greek thinkers alike said it was procreation. One suspects that the great majority of Christian lay people thought the same. But the small élite who wrote books and built up the tradition of the Church had a different view: procreation has lost its purpose in a world that is drawing towards its close and is already fully populated; we should concentrate all our efforts on a new form of procreation – Christian evangelization, as the spiritual procreation of new sons and daughters of God. Even Augustine repeated the quaint theme, often repeated in the early centuries, that sexual abstinence not only pointed to the age to come, where 'they neither marry nor are given in marriage' (MATTHEW 22:30), but would hasten its coming.

This denigration of physical procreation led many early Christians to renounce marriage; it certainly meant that a different justification had to be found for it. St Paul gave the answer: those who cannot exercise self-control should marry, since it is better to marry than to burn with passion (1 CORINTHIANS 7:9). To renounce sex altogether is the ideal, but it is beyond the power of most people. What they must do is keep sex within marriage; only within marriage can they satisfy the sexual urge without sin. This rather negative justification of marriage had the effect of putting sexual desire right at the centre of the stage.

Concupiscence

To sum up, early Christian teaching, going back to Jesus himself, promoted the ideal of single-mindedness, of the love of God as the only proper motive for action. This led Christians to be negative towards those instinctive bodily drives, particularly sex and aggression, that do not arise from a love of God, and pull the will in contrary directions. This traditional teaching was reinforced for Augustine by his doctrine of original sin. We saw in the last chapter how he gave a new emphasis to this doctrine in order to bring out our total dependence on divine grace. We shall now see how he developed the doctrine further by making original sin the cause of the sexual drive in fallen man.

Augustine observed the tragic contrast between the ideal of single-mindedness and the situation in which we human beings now find ourselves. Before the Fall man possessed self-mastery – complete control over his mind and body. In rebelling against God, he set up a rebellion within himself, a corruption of his nature that we call 'original sin'. A man's will is now the uneasy president of a republic in anarchy; equivalent to disobedient subjects in a state are the instinctive drives within the body. These drives do not arise from the desires of the soul or indeed from any rational choice whatsoever. Some of our natural drives, for instance towards self-preservation, are obviously useful. But many of them not only arise independently of the will but cannot be controlled by it. They frustrate our desire to shape our lives according to our ideals; they drive us into wrong acts. Augustine's term for these negative drives in man, not sinful in themselves but the cause of sin, is *concupiscence.*

In Augustine's view the supreme example of concupiscence is the sexual drive in fallen man. Not only is the sexual urge extremely strong and a frequent cause of wrongdoing, but the very facts of physiology have a lesson to tell. A whole tradition of bawdy poetry had celebrated the fact that males get erections when they don't want them, and can equally fail to get them when they do. The theme had been treated by pagan poets as an object of smutty humour; it was now picked by Augustine (who need not, of course, have read the poetry) as a vivid example of the way in which concupiscence resists the will. It was also an excellent illustration, or so it appeared, of the truth of his teaching about original sin. The facts of sexual physiology have nothing to do with the sins of the individual: they are part of our inheritance from Adam. Meanwhile, the female equivalent to the lack of genital control in the male is the agony of childbirth – something which had been treated as a penalty for the Fall of Man already in the Book of Genesis (3:16). Women experience appalling labour pains, and sometimes expire in giving birth.

If the behaviour of our sexual organs results from original sin, it follows that it must have been very different before the Fall and, were it not for original sin, would be very different now. According to the Bible, Adam and Eve did not have intercourse before the Fall (GENESIS 4:1); and since human mortality is a penalty of the Fall, it was the Fall that made procreation necessary for the survival of the race. As a result, many theologians in the early Church argued that, had it not been for the Fall, there would have been no procreation and no sexual intercourse. Augustine, on the contrary, held that God's commandment to the first human beings, 'Increase and multiply' (GENESIS 1:2), applied even before the Fall. Even though in fact the Fall took place before Adam and Eve had got round to procreating, they would have had children if they had stayed in paradise. But their experience of procreation would have been different from that of fallen humanity: women would have given birth without danger or labour pains, and the sexual organs would have been as obedient to the will as are our arms and legs.

Here Augustine has been accused of fantasizing, but he was able to argue that the possibility of total control over the sexual organs is supported by observed physiological fact. For even now some people possess an amazing control over their bodies:

There are some people who can even move their ears, either one at a time or both together. There are others who, without moving their heads, can shift their whole scalp of hair down to the forehead and back again at will. There are some who can swallow an incredible number of various articles and then by gently pressing their stomachs can produce, as if out of a bag, any article they please, in perfect condition. There are others who imitate the sounds of birds and animals or of other men so closely that one could not tell the difference without seeing them. Some people produce at will such musical sounds from their bottoms (without making a smell) that they seem to be singing from that part of their bodies. (C 14.24)

In fallen man, however, the sexual organs resist this degree of control. This makes human sexuality, as we experience it, a prime example of the effects of original sin. But its link to original sin is closer still: it is through sexual intercourse as tainted by concupiscence that original sin is passed down from generation to generation. In the very act of procreation, however worthy the motives of the couple, the sexual organs go their own wicked way. The very mode of intercourse both expresses and passes on the impotence of the human will and the power of concupiscence. As Augustine claims with a skilful use of a difficult biblical story, it is precisely because Jesus, according to the gospels, was born of a virgin without sexual intercourse that he, alone of the human race, was free of original sin.

The whole argument was for the Pelagians, with their rejection of original sin, as a red rag to a bull. Augustine's claim that the physiology of sexual intercourse and childbirth had been perverted by the Fall seemed particularly implausible. The greatest of his Pelagian opponents, Julian of Eclanum (d. after 440), argued that sexual desire is necessary for procreation and is therefore natural and healthy; he was ready to attribute it even to Christ himself. Julian argued that labour pains are not a penalty for original sin but, like sexual desire, a necessary part of the natural order. The same is true, he added, of all kinds of physical misfortunes, including death itself: man was mortal from his creation, and the 'death' that is the penalty of sin is not physical death but the death of the soul. This contrasted sharply with the position of Augustine, who understood the biblical account of the Fall (GENESIS 3:16-19) to imply that before it human beings were not subject to disease or death.

On this question – whether the physical ills of life are natural or the penalty of original sin – a modern critic is likely to side with Julian, but one can see the appeal of Augustine's position. It is inadequate as an answer to the problem of physical evil to say that it is part of the natural order, and life would be unimaginable without it; in face of the sorrows and tragedies of life such an argument is cold comfort indeed. A theologian who wishes to reconcile our experience of life to our belief that God made the world has to offer something more satisfying.

But to return to sexual desire, the contrast between the Pelagian claim that it is natural and Augustine's insistence that it results from original sin makes Augustine, if you like, more negative about sexuality than the Pelagians; it does not imply that his rules for the use of our sexuality were more restrictive. Julian claimed that sexual desire can, and should, be controlled by the will. In contrast, Augustine conceded to human weakness that men and women, without a very special gift of grace, cannot suppress their sexual drives; they need to exercise them, and this they do without sin if they restrict sex to marriage. Ideally, all sex ought to be for the purpose of procreation. But such is the strength of the sexual drive that married couples are likely to have intercourse for the purpose of satisfying and assuaging their sexual urges. This is, of course, a sin; but if they only have sex within marriage and do not exclude procreation, their sin is only a minor one, easily forgiven. And a spouse who has sex to satisfy not merely his own desire but that of his partner is paying the 'debt' he owes his partner, which is an act of justice as well as a kindness: 'Married persons are granted as a concession the right to demand from each other the payment of the conjugal debt even if they make an uncontrolled use of it' (Go 11.12).

Writing on marital sex, Augustine seems to imply that sex within marriage always involves lust; this arises from simple physiological fact, as well as from the mixed motives of even the most virtuous of couples. As a result, marital sex almost always contains an element of sin. Augustine's Pelagian opponents rejected this firmly, and accused him of an hostility to the body deriving from his Manichaean phase. But this misses the point: his concern was not to make people renounce sex but to allow them to practise it. The ideal may indeed be sexual renunciation, but this does not mean that sex even within marriage stands condemned; for life on earth cannot be wholly guided by ideals. This position is typical of Augustine's sober realism on all matters of morality.

Theologians today criticize him more strongly still. Sexual intercourse, they claim, is not only good on the physical plain but even has spiritual value: it expresses and promotes marital love – that love which shares in God's love for us. The present writer remembers from his school days a preacher who claimed that marital sex, being both loving and creative, was, of all human activities, the one where we are closest to God. In theory this may be true, but let's be more realistic about human motives: it would be fatuous to suppose that in actual fact most Christian couples engage in sex with the prime intention of expressing spiritual ideals. Augustine allows sexuality to be what it is – something instinctive and earthy.

The Indissolubility of Marriage

Although, as we have seen, Jesus' teaching on single-mindedness had implications for sexuality, his teaching directly relating to marriage lies elsewhere, in his prohibition of divorce and re-marriage: 'Everyone who divorces his wife and marries another is an adulterer; and he who marries a woman divorced from her husband commits adultery' (LUKE 16:18, probably the original form of the saying recorded slightly differently in MATTHEW 5:32 and MARK 10:11-12). The disciples, we are told, reacted with shock, not to say disbelief: 'If that is the problem between a man and his wife, it is surely better not to marry' (MATTHEW 19:10). But, as is shown by the history of the interpretation of this saying of

Jesus', the problem is less its apparent severity than its evident obscurity. The saying clearly states that divorce is a deplorable thing; no one who believes in marriage is likely to disagree. But the precise meaning of the saying was far from obvious to the Christians of the early centuries: it was not obvious that the prohibition was absolute and unconditional, it was unclear in what sense Jesus called remarriage 'adultery', and it was open to question whether the same rules should apply to both men and women.

A variety of answers to these questions is already implied in the New Testament passages that record or reflect this saying, and they tend to interpret it in a way that reduces its severity. The Gospel of Matthew allows a husband to divorce an adulterous spouse and marry again (5:32;19:9), as also, by implication, does St Paul (1 CORINTHIANS 7:11). But these texts do not allow a wife to do likewise; lifelong fidelity to a single spouse was seen as a virtue incumbent on women rather than men. The so-called 'double standard' – a strict rule for women and a lenient one for men – was enshrined, in different ways, in both Jewish and in Roman law, and most early Christians took it for granted.

Although this double standard appears to have been the most common form of marriage discipline in the early Christian communities, there was, as we might expect, considerable variation. We find evidence of a stricter rule, excluding all divorce and remarriage, and evidence too of a more lenient one, allowing women to remarry as well as men. Civil law in both Jewish and Graeco-Roman society allowed easy divorce and had no problems over remarriage; the churches appear to have concentrated on discouraging divorce on inadequate grounds, rather than attempting to prevent remarriage, particularly for men.

From the fourth century there was a gradual parting of ways between eastern and western Christendom in their rules over marriage. In the east the churches increased the possibility of divorce and remarriage by extending the grounds for divorce, and allowing wives as well as husbands to divorce their spouses. But, in the west, development was in the opposite direction: Augustine and a number of his contemporaries started a new campaign to prohibit remarriage even after divorce on good grounds, and to impose on men the same restrictions that applied to women. So both east and west came to reject the double standard, but while the east did so in the interests of leniency the west did so in the interests of rigorism.

Such rigorism was not entirely new, but the argumentation was. Earlier rigorists had simply stated, in the main, that remarriage had been forbidden by Christ. Augustine and his allies argued that so-called second marriages are not merely forbidden but impossible: a first marriage cannot be dissolved, even by separation and legal divorce; as long as both spouses in the first marriage remain alive, a 'second marriage' is a case of 'bigamy' (an attempt to have two spouses) and therefore invalid. The claim widely accepted by Christians since the time of the Gospel of Matthew, that adultery justifies divorce and remarriage, was ruled out of court: remarriage, so far from being justified by adultery, is itself a form of adultery. The marriage bond not only should not but cannot be dissolved, by any cause other than the death of one of the spouses.

This doctrine of the indissolubility of marriage was Augustine's own creation. Since the teaching was new it was naturally controversial, and debate continued for centuries. As late as AD 826 a Roman pope and council gave permission for the husband of an adulterous wife to divorce and remarry. But from the eleventh century the western Church was unanimous in upholding Augustine's teaching on the indissolubility of marriage, and this remains the teaching of the Roman Catholic Church even today. The churches of the Protestant Reform have generally returned to the Gospel of Matthew in allowing divorce and remarriage after adultery by one's spouse, while excluding the double standard of the early centuries that had restricted this concession to men.

That Augustine on this subject was a rigorist, even at a time when most of the Church was not, may come as a surprise, in view of his deep understanding of human weakness, as shown in his doctrine of original sin. But in his eyes it was one thing to stress original sin and quite another to ignore Christ's explicit teaching on marriage. Sinners are to be tolerated within the Church, but this did not mean that adultery can now count as marriage. Augustine the pastor will have seen the attraction of the lenient stance of the Gospel of Matthew, but Augustine the scriptural scholar argued that we cannot take it as the teaching of Christ: it is only found in Matthew, and the double standard on which it depends is unacceptable in a Christian Church where 'there is neither male nor female, but you are all one person in Christ Jesus' (GALATIANS 3:28).

Augustine's interpretation of Christ's teaching on divorce remains open to question. In calling remarriage 'adultery' Christ is more likely to have been giving a broad interpretation to the Sixth Commandment ('You shall not commit adultery') than pronouncing on validity. His resonant saying, 'What God has yoked together let not man divide' (MATTHEW 19:6), ought strictly to mean that a marriage *can* but *should not* be dissolved, since there is no point in forbidding the impossible. But this is to interpret Christ's words too strictly. Only one point is clear: he forbade divorce and remarriage. Augustine's interpretation has at least the merit of making sense of this prohibition.

It is also easy to criticize him for losing touch with reality. In Roman law common life and mutual affection constituted marriage; once a couple had separated, the marriage was at an end. His insistence that even after separation the marriage still continues may remind us of the Cheshire Cat in Lewis Carroll's *Alice in Wonderland*, which was able to vanish while leaving its grin behind. The doctrine of indissolubility implies that the essence of marriage is not common life or mutual affection; instead, it is some invisible bond, independent of observable reality.

What is this bond supposed to be? Augustine had no clear answer. But he was able to illustrate the power of the bond from the understanding of the Christian sacraments that he had developed during the Donatist controversy. The bond of baptism unites a Christian to the Church even if his life provides no evidence of real commitment; the holy few who are faithful to the norms of the Church are not the only members of the Church. Likewise, those couples who remain together are not the only couples joined in marriage:

Just as the sacrament of regeneration remains in someone who has been excommunicated for a crime, and he does not lose this sacrament even if he is never reconciled with God, so also the bond of the marital compact remains in a wife who has been divorced on the ground of fornication, and she does not lose this bond even if she is never reconciled with her husband. (Ad 2.4)

Augustine's teaching of the indissolubility of marriage, like that of the Roman Catholic Church today, can sound negative and restrictive. But what he was actually doing was attributing to Christian marriage a new dignity. Despite his bleak view of marital sex, discussed above, he recognized in marriage what he called 'a sacramental element', arising from its indissolubility. Fidelity in marriage was obedience to a commandment of Christ's, but it was more than that: it was the acknowledgement of a bond real though unseen, akin to the grace bestowed at baptism and confirmed in the eucharist. This kinship, as Augustine pointed out, adds force to the teaching of St Paul that marital love should imitate Christ's love for his Church (EPHESIANS 5:25): can we not say that Christian marriage is a sign and symbol of this love?

The medieval Church, developing this insight further, came to recognize marriage as itself a sacrament. The new churches of the Reformation rejected this: they reserved the word 'sacrament' to the two great sacraments (baptism and the eucharist) introduced by Christ himself. But is this more than a dispute over words? Catholics and Protestants alike recognize the spiritual character of Christian marriage. Marriage is a natural phenomenon, not a specifically Christian one, but within the Church it takes on a new meaning. The greatest mystery of the Christian religion is its message that God has 'elected' (chosen) us unconditionally to be his sons and daughters; sin can deprive us of the benefits of our election but can never cancel it. This love between God and his chosen people, between Christ and his Church, would seem so extraordinary as to beggar belief, were it not for the continuing expression of this bond in Christian marriage. Here husband and wife give themselves to each other unconditionally and for life, in imitation of the unconditional love of God.

How much of this is in Augustine? Certainly he proclaimed the indissolubility of marriage, and linked it to the role of marriage in symbolizing the love of God. He thereby laid the foundations for the high evaluation of marriage developed after his time into one of the glories of the Christian tradition. This was a major contribution to Christian thought.

However, he is open to criticism in one respect: he says too much about the indissolubility of marriage even after divorce, and not enough about the value of the bond of love that unites husband and wife in a successful marriage: surely the latter is the clearer symbol of the reality of Christ's love for his Church? One has to admit that Augustine has little to say about the companionate side of marriage – the intimate fellowship and mutual support between husband and wife in a lifelong union. This was partly because of his concern to argue that marriage survives the breakdown of such a union, but there was another reason as well: he did not see this aspect of marriage as its distinguishing feature. Lifelong bonds of love are found within marriage but also in many other human relationships – in friendship, and in community life at its best. It is Augustine's teaching on friendship and community that will be the subject of my next and final chapter.

6

Friendship and Community

Augustine's conception of the Church and its place in the world has been one of the main themes of this book. Augustine takes for granted that the Church is an institution with its own organs of government, rules and procedures, but what interests him as a theologian is the Church as community, and community conceived in terms not of rights and obligations but of human relationships. This chapter will explore how he developed a concept of community in the Church that built on his own strong feelings of attachment towards individuals.

Love of Persons

A recurrent theme in the *Confessions* is friendship, or the love between persons. At least until he went to Hippo, Augustine was always in a circle of close friends, with whom he shared without inhibition or reserve every detail of his personal life and each development of his thoughts.

> *All kinds of things absorbed my mind in their company – to make conversation, share a joke, do each other acts of kindness; read pleasant books together, pass from making jokes to talk of the deepest things and back again; disagree without ill feeling, as a man might debate with himself, and find our harmony all the sweeter for the occasional disagreement; teach one another and learn from one another; long*

> *with impatience for the return of the absent, and welcome them back*
> *with joy. These and other signs came from the very heart as we gave*
> *and received affection. Produced by the face, the tongue, the eyes and a*
> *thousand pleasant gestures, they acted as fuel to set our minds on fire*
> *and out of many make us one.* (Co 4.8.13)

Augustine picked up, by experience illuminated by his reading of
Cicero, the ancient view of friendship as the greatest of human
blessings. The very strength of his feelings set him a problem
when as a Christian theologian he came to address the question of
the relation between the love of one's friends, the love of one's fellow men in general, and the love of God. How are these related to
each other, and what is the priority between them?

In a work called *Christian Teaching*, begun at the same time
as the *Confessions*, Augustine introduced a distinction between
enjoyment of God – a union with him in which we find complete
fulfilment – and the *use* we make of created beings, including our
fellow men, in our quest for God. Since created goods cannot
satisfy us, we cannot make them our final goal, and we cannot
properly be said to *enjoy* them for themselves. It was, of course, a
traditional theme that it is foolish to be attached to material things
for their own sake. Augustine has been criticized for treating love
of other human beings in the same way, as if we should exploit
them for our own spiritual benefit, without becoming too
attached to them, much as we make use of things. But he was well
aware of the distinction between the love of things and the love of
persons: as he wrote in another context, 'We should obviously not
love human beings as things to be consumed. Friendship is a kind
of benevolence, leading us to do things for the benefit of those we
love' (J 8.5). Augustine did not mean that we should moderate our
love for our fellow human beings and concentrate exclusively on
the love of God. The point he is making is simply that we must
avoid attributing to anything other than God a value in and of
itself, independent of God; instead, we should love our fellows 'in'

God. What did he mean by this? At this point the argument becomes intricate but also highly rewarding.

Augustine pointed out that even in loving ourselves we look to a goal that lies beyond ourselves, namely the love of God. This is because the love of God is necessary for our happiness but cannot be exploited as the means to an end: we find our happiness not as a *result* of loving God, but *in* loving him. Happiness is to be found not in self-absorption but in the contemplation of God, as an object of love for his own sake. If we attain this, self-love is satisfied in a way it would never be if we placed our final goal in ourselves and not in God.

In this way self-love, properly informed, fulfils the first of the great commandments: 'You are to love the Lord your God with all your heart, and with all your soul, and with all your mind' (MATTHEW 22:37). But there is also the second great commandment: 'You are to love your neighbour as yourself' (MATTHEW 22:39). Now if self-love points us to the love of God and we are to love our neighbour as ourselves, it follows that we should love him not in himself or for himself, but 'in God' or 'for the sake of God'. This is not to impose a restriction on love of neighbour – as if it is a good thing only is so far as it helps our love of God. No, the point being made is this: love of my neighbour means wanting him or her to share in my own aspiration towards God as the final goal.

Whatever else enters the mind as an object of love is to be swept along in the direction in which the whole current of our affections flows [the love of God]. Whoever has a proper love for his neighbour ought to act towards him in such a way that he too comes to love God with his whole heart and soul and mind. For in this way, loving his neighbour as himself, a man pours all his love both of himself and of his neighbour into the love of God which allows no streams to be diverted away from itself. (CT 1.22.21)

Augustine rightly perceives that true love for a fellow human being does not consist in adoration of that person as he or she is, in a form of aesthetic contemplation. Human beings are beings in movement towards God their goal, and to love your neighbour is to want him to attain that goal. To love someone as he is, in the sense of making him an object of adoration (whether in hero worship or romantic love), is to close one's eyes to the actual reality of a human being who, so far from being satisfied with himself as he is, aspires towards a perfection he has not yet attained. True love involves true sympathy, in which the lover perceives that aspiration and makes it his own as well; to love your neighbour as yourself is to want both him and you to achieve your common goal. Augustine argues this convincingly. Having started with a confusing distinction between objects of enjoyment and objects of use, he achieves a correct conception of love of persons, a love distinct both from the desire to possess and the impulse to adore.

Apart from the relation between love of God and love of neighbour, there is also the problem of the relation of universal love to particular loves: we have a call to love all our fellow human beings; we also recognize a particular obligation to help our families and friends. How are these two related? Is there conflict between them? Pagan moralists, such as Cicero, had deplored wronging one's fellow citizens to help one's nearest and dearest, or wronging foreigners to help one's fellow citizens. But the problem becomes particularly acute for a Christian, because Christ's commandment to love one's neighbour as oneself seems to mean that one should treat even strangers as if they were friends.

Augustine understood Christ to mean that we must love all people equally. 'But since', he added, 'you cannot do good to all, you are to pay special attention to those with whom you enjoy closer contact because of the dictates of place, time and other circumstances' (CT 1.28.29). Yes, we are right to give priority to our nearest and dearest: 'A man has responsibility above all towards his own people. Obviously, both in the order of nature and in that of human society he has better access to them and a greater opportunity to attend to their needs' (C 19.14). 'Better access' is pretty weak as an explanation of the special duties each one of us has towards the members of his or her own family, but at least Augustine is trying give these duties a place in a Christian ethic of love of neighbour.

He came up with a better answer through further reflection on the nature of Christian love. Such love shares in the love of God towards his creatures, a love in which there is pure giving and no thought of getting anything in return, since God in the perfection of his being is in need of nothing. But since human beings share lacks and needs, love between human beings involves 'bearing one another's burdens' (GALATIANS 6:2 – a favourite text of Augustine's). Ideally, all human beings should help one another, and in the world to come we may look forward to a union of all the saints in knowledge and love of each other; but in the conditions of this present world this is simply not possible, and in most of our relationships there is a lack of full mutuality. Growth in Christian love requires each of us to build his own circle of friends, who love one another as themselves and help one another to grow in the love of God. This ideal of friendship gave Augustine a special interest in the development of religious community; here more than anywhere he hoped that true Christian fellowship could be realized on earth.

The Ideal of Community Life

Even before his conversion at Milan in 386 (treated in the opening section of my first chapter) Augustine was attracted by the idea of setting up a community where he and his closest friends could devote themselves to study and reflection. An initial scheme envisaged around ten companions coming together and pooling all their resources to create a common fund; but some of those hoping to join were married, and their wives rejected the scheme. But soon afterwards Augustine was bowled off his feet when he learnt about the monastic movement, started by Antony of Egypt. After a fierce inward struggle, he decided to give up his career and prospects of marriage, and devote himself to a life of chastity, prayer and reflection, out of a wish, to use his own quaint phrase, 'to become like God in a life of retirement' (L 10.2).

Accompanied by his little band of friends and followers, Augustine returned to Africa in 388 in order to start a monastic community in his native town of Thagaste, the first in the province of Africa. It was on a visit to Hippo in 391 to see a potential recruit that he was forced to accept ordination to the priesthood. This did not mean the end of his monastery: it simply joined him in Hippo. When a few years later (in 396) he became bishop of the see, he set up a parallel community for his clergy: distinguished from the lay monastery by their active ministry, they too had to renounce personal property.

Augustine wrote a rule for the lay monastery. Subsequently, both in the Middle Ages and in modern times, this rule was adopted by many orders and communities; it is at present followed by more priests, monks and nuns than the better-known Rule of St Benedict. This document, together with a number of letters and sermons, presents a clear picture of Augustine's ideal of community life. What were its essential features?

Augustine's favourite biblical text on this theme was the brief account in the Acts of the Apostles of the life of the primitive Christian community at Jerusalem: 'Now the multitude of those who believed had one heart and soul, and no one said that any of the things he possessed was his own, but they had everything in common' (ACTS 4:32). Modern commentators tell us that this common ownership was not a form of primitive communism but simply generous contributions from the wealthier members of the community to a fund for its poor members. But in the new monastic communities of the fourth century, with their strict rules of communal ownership, this text was taken more literally and often quoted. No one made fuller use of it than Augustine. He insisted in the communities he founded that all the members should renounce personal ownership. Those who possessed property were to hand it over to their relations or give it to the community. Even clothes were to be possessed in common: they were to be regularly returned to a common store for redistribution. Private property, he knew, is divisive and a fertile source of quarrels; it is necessary in the outside world where people have families and dependants to support, but it has no place in a religious community.

Even more important in Augustine's eyes than the sharing of material goods was the sharing of thoughts, concerns and feelings. He pointed out that spiritual, or mental, goods – joy, wisdom, the love of God, and so on – are vastly superior to material ones in two ways: first, they will continue into the life to come, while material goods will pass away; secondly, they can be shared in a way material goods cannot. When a number of people divide up among themselves material goods such as money or clothing, each receives only a portion, and the greater the number of people taking part, the smaller the share received by each one. In contrast,

> someone's possession of goodness is in no way diminished by the arrival, or the continuance, of a sharer in it; indeed, goodness is a possession enjoyed more widely if those who possess it are united in harmonious fellowship. In fact, anyone who refuses to share this possession with others will not enjoy it at all; and he will find that his possession of it will be in precise proportion to his readiness to love his partner in it. (C 15.5)

So spiritual goods, unlike material ones, are not diminished by being more widely distributed: they are actually increased.

Feelings such as joy or love are intensified when shared with others. Even where there is perfect mutual sympathy and concern for the needs of others the fact remains that human beings are in competition when it comes to material comforts. It is only mental and spiritual riches – rejoicing with those who rejoice, sharing ideas and enthusiasms with one's fellows – that really bind communities together. It is only when spiritual goods are treasured, and material goods put into second place, that fellowship free of envy and rivalry can develop.

But it is not only material things that cause division: personal ties of kinship can do the same. As Augustine wrote to a monk who was tempted to leave his monastery to look after his mother,

The rule that everyone is to renounce all his possessions involves hating one's father and mother, wife and children, brothers and sisters, and even one's own life too [CF. LUKE 14:26]. For all these things are personal possessions, which generally get in the way of attaining not indeed those personal possessions that will pass away with time but those lasting and eternal goods that we shall possess in common. Having a particular woman as your mother is something you cannot share with me; and accordingly it is temporary and will pass away ... But having a sister in Christ is something that can be shared by both of us, and by all who are promised in the same union of love the one heavenly inheritance with God as our Father and Christ as our brother. This is eternal and will never be eroded by the passing of time; this we may hope to retain all the more firmly, the more we declare it is to be possessed not privately but in common ... Each person is to think the same about his own soul. Let each man hate to have a feeling he cannot share with others, for such a feeling must belong to what passes away; let each man love in his soul that communion and sharing of which it is written, 'They had towards God one soul and one heart' [CF. ACTS 4:32]. So your soul is not your own, but belongs to all the brethren; and their souls are yours. Or rather, your soul and theirs make up not many souls but one soul – the single mind of Christ. (I. 243)

Augustine rejects an individualism that sees thoughts and feelings as the property of separate and independent minds; he insists instead that they are developed through contact with others and are naturally shared with them. The happiness of the saints in heaven consists in a common enjoyment of union with God, where souls will be perfectly open to each other and share the same spiritual life. Augustine has a similar vision of happiness on earth. Perfect knowledge and love of one another cannot, it is true, be attained in this life, because of our selfishness and our imperfect understanding even of ourselves, let alone of other people; but the approach to such a marriage of true minds remains the greatest happiness attainable on earth.

What Augustine has done is to apply in a new context the concept of friendship traditional in pagan literature – with its talk of friends having a single soul, through complete harmony in pursuits, aims and convictions. Pagan society thought this ideal realizable only between a man and a tiny circle of his closest friends. Augustine applies this ideal of friendship to the new context of Christian fellowship, where all members of the Church are united by a common goal and need the assistance of one another to attain it. Christianity stimulates joint action where the whole company of believers is united by a common aspiration that inspires the actions of each one. Actions cease to express the individual will of the agent and to be his responsibility alone: instead, they become the realization of choices that the agent shares with his fellows.

This ideal of shared will and thought and action had been powerfully developed by Aristotle (fourth century BC) in the context of personal friendships between members of the Athenian upper class (see A. W. Price, *Love and Friendship in Plato and Aristotle*, Chapter 4). What Augustine did was to enrich this ideal with the biblical theme of life in Christ, and apply it to the Christian community. Since in practice the members of the Christian Church are divided by social barriers and those clashes of interest that are inevitable in the secular world, this fellowship is best realized in small communities, where the members know each other intimately, share the same aspirations, and work together to achieve them for all. This creates a life of common loyalties, feelings, hopes and goals, where all the members imitate Christ and become, through union with him, one heart and one soul.

Augustine's Originality

How original was Augustine's ideal of community life? Friendship certainly had a part to play in the new monastic movement, which developed in the Greek east in the early fourth century and spread to the Latin west in Augustine's lifetime. This monastic movement was inspired by a wish to escape from the social pressures of secular life in order to develop the inner life of self-knowledge and openness to God. But this does not mean that monks aimed at total self-sufficiency or sacrificed all social ties to the quest for mystical communion with God. The literature of eastern monasticism reveals anxiety over wrong forms of friendship, leading to possessiveness or mutual admiration societies, and is more concerned to stress the negative virtues of patience and tolerance than to promote positive ideals of friendship. Nevertheless close relations between monks are taken for granted, and numerous sayings and anecdotes illustrate how helpful a true friend can be.

Once the monastic movement began to attract educated recruits who knew the classical ideal of friendship, we would anticipate a richer development of this theme. But this occurred more slowly than we might expect. Basil of Caesarea (d. 379), who had received a full secular education and whose writings enjoy a unique status in Orthodox monasticism, wrote eloquently of the need for community if monks are to learn from each other and practise the active virtues. Particularly interesting is his claim that 'many commandments are easily performed by a number living together but not by someone living on his own' *(LONGER RULES*

7): this implies that in a community each member shares responsibility for the actions of his fellows. This insight is similar to Augustine's but is not developed.

Augustine's western contemporary John Cassian (d. around 435), spent, or claimed to have spent, many years in monastic communities in Egypt and Palestine, and later wrote a great series of *Conferences* to apply the insights of eastern monasticism to the needs of the Latin west. His *Conference 16*, on friendship, emphasizes the need to be ready to sacrifice one's personal interests and even opinions in order to keep one's friends. He is more precise, and arguably more realistic, than Augustine about the difficulties of maintaining trust and harmony within a community. But this does not change the fact that, like Basil, he falls far short of Augustine's vision.

In all, the early monastic tradition in both east and west was emphatic on the value of friendship even for contemplative monks living apart from the world, but Augustine was original in seeing beyond the simple notion of harmony between the brethren, and developing the ideal of a shared mental life of common aspirations, thoughts and feelings. It is typical of him that he explained the very word 'monk' (whose root, the Greek word *monos*, means 'alone') as deriving from the emphasis in Acts 4:32 on oneness of heart and soul. For Augustine true happiness consists in overcoming the separation between distinct human minds and creating a spiritual life developed and enjoyed by a number of friends together. In this way life on earth can imitate, however imperfectly, the communion of saints in heaven.

The theme that monastic life imitates and anticipates the life of heaven was already a traditional one in Augustine's time. It was linked to ideals of sinlessness, emotional stability, and the vision of God. It was Augustine who played down these ascetic and mystical elements in favour of the ideal of a life of shared mental experience, of an overcoming of the separateness of human souls through a common raising of heart and mind to God.

The climax of the *Confessions* is arguably the so-called 'Vision at Ostia' (9.10.23–26) – a mystical experience, momentary but unforgettable, in which Augustine, shortly before returning to Africa, achieved a sense of transcending the created order and tasting the eternity of God. Most unusually for a mystical experience it was not a solitary one: he shared it with his mother, Monica. His belief in the possibility of overcoming the opaqueness of human minds to each other, and developing a mental world of shared experience, was not the romantic dream of a man unable to come to terms with the loneliness and isolation that separate human beings: it was born of an experience of warm human relations with his family and friends, and of a conviction that life in this world can receive a real if faint imprint of its goal – the communion of saints and union with God himself.

Imitating the Trinity

The Christian God is not some philosophical Absolute, so transcendent and pure in essence that he is unrelated to other beings: instead, he is intimately linked in love to the human beings he has created. Moreover, he is himself one God in three persons, Father, Son and Holy Spirit, united to each other in a bond of love. This enabled Augustine to relate his ideal of perfect human community to the Christian doctrine of God.

Augustine devoted to this doctrine one of his longest works – the fifteen books of *The Trinity*, which he worked at on and off for two decades (the 400s and 410s). In this work he insists that there are not three beings in God but a single reality or 'substance'. He had to accept the traditional formulation that Father, Son and Holy Spirit are three 'persons', but he insisted that the word 'person' in this context has no particular meaning: 'we say "three persons" not in order to say precisely that, but in order not to be reduced to silence' (T 5.9.10). Three 'persons' suggests, in ordinary language, three separate individuals with three different minds and three different wills: but in God there is only a single mind and a single will.

What, then, is the threefold element in the Trinity? For Augustine, the answer lies in the *relations* between Father, Son and Spirit. The relations in question are those of source and derivation: the Father is the source from whom the Son derives his being, while the Spirit derives his being from both the Father and the Son. Normally when we say a number of persons are related to each other, we mean that they exist as separate individuals who, as a distinct fact, are linked through being related to each other. But in the case of the Trinity, according to Augustine, relation has precisely the opposite function: it does not link what is otherwise distinct, but sets apart what in all other respects is indistinguishable. The persons are distinct *only* in being related to each other. The Son, in deriving his being from the Father, is necessarily distinct from the Father; but in every other respect, in mind and will, in qualities and activities, he is one and the same being. The same is true of the Holy Spirit, in deriving his being from the Father and the Son. In this way we distinguish the Father from the Son, and the Holy Spirit from both, while maintaining a strong doctrine of divine unity.

The fact that this account of the Trinity became standard in the west should not dull us to its extreme oddity. Augustine, in effect, invented a new and bizarre concept of relationship. The result was unfortunate: under his influence the doctrine of the Trinity became so artificial and so hard to grasp that it ceased to be part of the religion of the faithful, and retreated into the study of the professional theologian.

But in the context of Augustine's theme of Christian community his account of the Trinity takes on a new relevance. Most obviously, the oneness of will within the Trinity is a perfect model for the unity of wills in Christian community: as Father, Son and Holy Spirit possess in common a single will, so human beings are called to a perfect harmony of will, through sharing together the same desire to achieve union with God.

But Augustine's favourite argument relates not to the mere oneness of will in the Trinity but to the rooting of that oneness in a bond of love. The three persons of the Trinity form a single divine reality, or substance, with one mind and one will, but there remain distinctions between them: this means that the unity between them is to be defined not merely as identity of substance but as a bond of love, comparable to love between human persons. The Holy Spirit, in proceeding from both the Father and the Son, as the common source of the Spirit, can be called the bond of love that unites them. Augustine draws out the implications this has for human beings:

> *We are bidden to imitate this bond by grace, in our relationships both with God and with one another, in the two precepts [love of God and love of neighbour] on which the whole law and the prophets depend [MATTHEW 22:40]. In this way those three [Father, Son, and Holy Spirit] are one God, unique, great, wise, holy, and blessed. And we find our blessedness 'from him and through him and in him' [ROMANS 11:36], because it is by his gift that we are one with each other.* (T 6.5.7.)

In this passage Augustine begins with the theme of love within God – note that the phrase 'from him and through him and in him' is itself a Trinitarian formula. He then proceeds downwards, as it were, to the theme of love between human beings. But it is just as possible to reason in the opposite direction – to start with human love, and then move upwards to the love that unites the persons of the Trinity. This is really a better procedure, since it is precisely our human experience of love that enables us to gain some conception of divine love. It is the procedure adopted in the eighth book of *The Trinity*, where Augustine offers the following analysis of human love.

If I love my neighbour, I am conscious of the feeling of love and attach value to it. I can say that in loving my neighbour I love love itself. Three realities come together – the one who loves, the one who is loved, and the love that unites them. Moreover, since God is love, to love love is to love God. So my human experience of love of neighbour provides a mirror, or image, of God himself; and moreover this experience contains a threefold element, or trinity, that bears a resemblance to the divine Trinity itself. To use Augustine's own words:

> 'Yes, [someone will say,] I can see love and, as far as I can, conceive it in my mind; and I believe the scripture when it says that "God is love and whoever abides in love abides in God" [1 JOHN 4:16]. But when I see it, I don't see the Trinity in it.' Oh but you do see the Trinity if you see love ... For love stems from someone in love, and it is with love that someone or something is loved. Here we have three things – the lover, the object of his love, and love. (T 8.8.12–10.14)

Since the Holy Spirit is called in Scripture both the Spirit of the Father and the Spirit of the Son, and since he derives his being from both Father and Son, and is sent into the hearts of human beings by the Father and the Son acting together, it follows that he is the bond linking Father and Son. 'God is love' (1 JOHN 4:8), and within the Trinity it is supremely the Spirit who represents divine love: the Father and Son are lover and beloved, and the Spirit is the love that unites them. The Spirit is also the bond of love between God and his creatures: 'God's love has been poured into our hearts through the Holy Spirit that has been given to us' (ROMANS 5:5). It follows that Christian love is no less than a sharing in the Holy Spirit, in that bond of love that binds together the persons of the Trinity. In other words, Christian fellowship, as a union of love, is an image on earth of the Trinity; human community mirrors on earth the 'community' of the Trinity.

In the following part of the work (Book Nine) Augustine shifts the emphasis from this image of the Trinity in human community to a psychological one – the image of the Trinity within the human mind itself. Each human mind is a unity, since there is one 'self', and at the same time a plurality, since the mind performs all the time a variety of mental acts, especially the three acts of remembering, understanding and willing; this makes the mind like the Trinity itself, in which there is one substance and yet three persons. Augustine makes this shift from the community model of the Trinity to the psychological one for the following reason: the oneness in God is more fully echoed in the unity of a single human self than in the looser 'union' between a number of different human beings. Unfortunately, this has the effect of making the love that unites the Trinity look more like the self-love of a single individual than the Christian love of neighbour.

This does not mean, however, that Augustine went back on his teaching that love of neighbour echoes the love within God himself. Despite the unsatisfactory features in his doctrine of the Trinity, it remains the case that he saw a connection between the love that is the Spirit uniting Father and Son and the human love of neighbour perfected in Christian community. No reader of Augustine can fail to be struck by the real similarity between, on the one hand, his Trinitarian doctrine of three divine persons with one mind and will and, on the other, his ideal of community as described above – a union of friends who are one in heart and soul through sharing in fellowship the same thoughts, feelings and aspirations.

Conclusion

Augustine is not only the most prolific of the early Church Fathers but also the most wide-ranging. There are so many themes one could select as the heart of his message: I could have chosen, for example, his doctrine of the individual human being, made in the image of the Trinity, corrupted through the Fall, and refashioned through the grace of Christ; he does not preach community in a way that minimizes the value or responsibilities of the individual. Nevertheless, his stress on the community aspects of Christian life remains striking, and it has been the leading theme of this book. It arose partly from the influence of such African predecessors as Cyprian, with their emphasis on the doctrine of the Church, and partly as a response to the particular needs of his own time. But Augustine transcends his immediate context, and his treatment of Christian community remains a stimulus and a challenge even today. What, in sum, are its essential components?

We saw in chapter 1 how, according to Augustine, the basis of Christian teaching is the authority possessed by the Church as a community stretching back to the Apostles. Chapter 2 looked at Augustine's view of the Church as a community that binds together saints and sinners in a fellowship of sacrament and prayer. Chapter 3 treated his teaching on the relationship between the Church and the world, where, whatever the differences in motivation between sincere Christians and the rest of mankind, they are united by a common striving for peace. In chapter 4 we saw how, in the Augustinian doctrine of grace, human beings are united to each other through their equal dependence on the unmerited favour of God. Chapter 5 proceeded to Augustine's teaching on Christian marriage as the symbol, within a human relationship, of the love of Christ for his Church.

It is in his teaching on friendship and community that these themes find their richest development, in the notion of a shared spiritual life which heals and overcomes the isolation of the individual. Christian community on earth is a preparation for the communion of saints in heaven, where we shall be totally transparent one to another, and share the vision of God in union with each other. This, it transpires, is nothing less than a participation in the unity in plurality of the Holy Trinity itself. The deepest need of human beings is to be so transformed that we come to 'share in the very being of God' (2 PETER 1:5). To open ourselves to this transformation, we must grow in true fellowship, through developing bonds of mutual love and common hope. It is here, perhaps, that we today have most to learn from the message of Augustine.

Suggested Further Reading

Augustine's psychological perception and unusual self-knowledge make him one of the very few ancient writers whose works provide us with the material required for a modern biography. This has been provided by Peter Brown, *Augustine of Hippo,* University of California Press, 1967; though it is primarily an account of the life, quite exceptional for its insight and freshness, it includes discussion of most of the themes treated in this book. So does Gerald Bonner, *St Augustine of Hippo: Life and Controversies,* revised edition, AMS Press, 1985, which provides an admirably lucid, though uncritical, account of Augustine's case against Manichees, Donatists and Pelagians.

Meanwhile, Augustine the philosopher (and philosophical theologian) receives a sophisticated treatment from John M. Rist, *Augustine: Ancient Thought Baptized,* Cambridge University Press, 1994..Difficult but unusually stimulating is Christopher Kirwan, *Augustine,* Routledge, 1989, which does Augustine the welcome compliment of subjecting his ideas to sharp critical analysis.

There are excellent translations of the *Confessions* and the *City of God* in the Penguin Classics, by R. Pine-Coffin, 1961, and H. Bettenson, 1972, respectively; these two works are arguably the greatest of all Augustine's writings, but both are difficult reading for those unacquainted with ancient thought. The particular literary and historical problems of the *Confessions* receive a remarkably fresh and illuminating treatment in Gillian Clark, *Augustine: the Confessions,* Cambridge University Press, 1993. A reader who is impressed with my claim that it is immoral to condemn Pelagius without reading him should read *The Letters of Pelagius and his Followers,* translated and edited by B. R. Rees, Boydell & Brewer, 1991.

A new edition of the whole of Augustine — *The Works of St Augustine, A Translation for the 21st Century,* New City Press, New York — is in process of appearing, and already includes many volumes of sermons in a superbly racy translation. These sermons were largely preached extempore and taken down by shorthand writers at the time of delivery; this gives them a freshness and generally a simplicity that is likely to appeal to the modern reader more than the studied art of Augustine's more polished writings. Any volume of these sermons, plus the Brown biography as an overview, will provide the general reader with the wherewithal to enter more deeply into the mind of Augustine.

Two other books referred to in the main text of this volume and which may be of interest are: Aries, P. And Duby, G. eds, *A History of Private Life, Volume I: From Rome to Byzantium,* Harvard University Press, 1987; and Price, A. W., *Love and Friendship in Plato and Aristotle,* Oxford University Press, 1989.

Index